If You Really Loved Me

JASON EVERT

If You Really Loved Me

100 Questions on Dating, Relationships, and Sexual Purity

CATHOLIC ANSWERS
SAN DIEGO
2003

Published by Catholic Answers, Inc.
2020 Gillespie Way
El Cajon, California 92020
(888) 291-8000 (orders)
(619) 387-0042 (fax)
www.catholic.com (web)

Cover photo by Howard Decruyenaere
Cover design by Chris Gilbert, DesignWorks
Typesetting by Loyola Graphics

Printed in the United States of America
ISBN 1-888992-33-6

Dedication

For Mary

Acknowledgments

Thanks to my toughest editors—the high school and college students across the country who critiqued this manuscript for me. I offer you my thanks and prayers for making this book what it has become. Your input was invaluable to me: Crystalina Padilla, Kelly Evert, Christine Furasek, Caitlin Gillen, Brian H. Johnson, Kara and Alexandra Klein, Margaret McCullough, Tori Roberts, Lauren Savoy, Zach Werner, and Katie Yarger.

To Dr. Deregal Burbank, Dr. Ed Bessler, Anthony Zimmerman, Lloyd Duplatis, and all of the other medical experts who were more than generous in assisting and correcting my research. To Jimmy Akin, Trask Tapperson, Steven Greydanus, and Michelle Arnold who were also a blessing to this work.

Saving the best for last, to my mother and father, for all they have taught me about life and love and the difference between right and wrong. As a sign of my gratitude to them all, I ask anyone who has benefited from reading this book to offer a simple prayer for all of their intentions.

Contents

It is Jesus that you seek when you dream of happiness; he is waiting for you when nothing else you find satisfies you; he is the beauty to which you are so attracted; it is he who provokes you with that thirst for fullness that will not let you settle for compromise; it is he who urges you to shed the masks of a false life; it is he who reads in your hearts your most genuine choices, the choices that others try to stifle. It is Jesus who stirs in you the desire to do something great with your lives, the will to follow an ideal, the refusal to allow yourselves to be ground down by mediocrity, the courage to commit yourselves humbly and patiently to improving yourselves and society, making the world more human and more fraternal.[1]

—Pope John Paul II

~

Dear young people, have the sacred ambition to become holy like he is holy! Young people of every continent, do not be afraid to be the saints of the new millennium! May the gospel become your most precious treasure . . . may most holy Mary give you the strength and wisdom to be able to speak to God and of God.[2]

—Pope John Paul II

Introduction

Planned Parenthood recommends that to have a healthier sex life, you should "be selective when you choose a sex partner. . . . Be sure you know your partner's name *and* phone number."[3] *Newsweek* magazine reported that since female chimpanzees, grasshoppers, hyenas, dung flies, and penguins are sexually promiscuous, this may be evidence that such behavior is beneficial for women as well.[4]

I have been to the zoo on several occasions, but since I cannot recall seeing any hyenas that felt used after a broken sexual relationship, I would not recommend that you make any life-changing decisions based on *Newsweek*'s findings. The same is true for the advice of Planned Parenthood.

Our generation is ready for a better kind of love than Jerry Springer offers. The reason we hunger for direction in relationships becomes obvious when we consider the quality of advice the world gives. Medical professionals tell us how to avoid venereal infections, and *Cosmopolitan* magazine offers "lust lessons,"[5] but what we really want to know is how to find authentic, lasting love.

To find a different kind of advice, I read through the Bible as well as the writings of saints, physicians, philosophers, theologians, and marriage counselors. Based on that collective wisdom, this book addresses the one-hundred most common questions we have on dating, love, and the meaning of sex. I speak to about fifteen thousand high school and college students per month, and the following questions are nothing more than a collection of the best ones they have asked me.

I discovered, in researching this book, that the one key that seems to unlock the mystery of sexuality is reverence—purity of heart. When we become irreverent toward sex, we are blind to a reality that would take the world's breath away. As Christ said,

"Blessed are the pure in heart, for *they shall see God*" (Matt. 5:8). Through purity of heart, a man is able to see God's image in a woman, and a woman is able to see God's image in a man. We catch a glimpse of what Adam and Eve originally saw in each other, and we discover our vocation to love one another as God loves us. Since God created us to love as he does, to love with purity is to rediscover the meaning of life. Through purity of heart, for example, a man becomes aware that he is dealing with a daughter of the King of Heaven; in other words, a princess. The man's job is that of the knight, but a knight cannot be brave unless he has love. His love gives him the courage to honor his woman in such a way that if she died unexpectedly, he could place her in the arms of Jesus and say, "Here she is, my Lord. I took care of her."

This is love, and unless we embrace such a challenge we miss the whole point of life. As Pope John Paul II said, "Man cannot live without love. He remains a being that is incomprehensible for himself, his life is senseless, if love is not revealed to him, if he does not encounter love, if he does not experience it and make it his own, if he does not participate intimately in it. This is why Christ the Redeemer 'fully reveals man to himself.' "[6]

Christ crucified teaches us what it means to be human: That we will find ourselves only in the fullest giving of ourselves. For each person, this fullest giving of one's self will come in a unique way. For one, it may be the giving of one's self in marriage; for others, in the religious or the single life. All are called to make a sincere gift of themselves and in this way fulfill the very meaning of their existence.

I have not always appreciated the sacrificial nature of love. At more times than I would like to admit, I have tried to keep God's nose out of my business: "If only I can live this part of my life without him, then I'll have some freedom. How am I supposed to have a life otherwise?" If we harbor this thought, we have bought the biggest lie on earth: "God is holding out on us, and when it comes down to it, he does not want us to be happy and have love. If we want fulfillment, we need to forget God and the Church and grab it ourselves!" Essentially we are saying, "If only I can keep the Author of love out of my love life!"

To let God into our love lives, we must have the courage to listen to our conscience. This is an echo of the voice of God in our hearts, directing us to authentic love and telling us when we are selling ourselves short. At times we might suppress our conscience, seeing it as the enemy of freedom and love. But if we have the courage to follow it, we will have life and have it abundantly. It is ironic that we find the freedom and love we long for in the place we least expect—in obedience to God's laws.

Even those who click onto a pornographic web site are yearning for what only God's plan for love can fulfill. Everyone who gets drunk at a party and the next morning can not remember who he slept with is on the same quest. Though such people might seem uninterested in God, they are actually longing for him because behind every sexual desire and even every addiction is a yearning for God, a hunger to experience love in all its intensity. We all long for the kind of love for which we were made. The good news that Christ bears is that this love is possible (regardless of our past), and he is waiting for us to come to him so that we might receive it.

If we truly desire love, we must have the courage to take a deep look into the motives of our hearts and a deep look at the meaning of sex. Do we *really* want to know the truth about sex? Are we willing to hear the demands that authentic love places upon us? Part of the truth is the bad news: all of us are tempted to use others for our emotional or physical gratification. A battle exists in the heart between love and lust; those who experience true love will be the ones who wage war against the counterfeits we are all prone to embrace.

So what is the cost of following God's way? What is God asking of me when it comes to purity? Is it simply that I avoid adultery and X-rated movies? If I have the courage to listen to Christ, will he ask me to give him something that I am not ready to surrender? If we retreat from the challenge of looking honestly at our hearts, if we act as if there is no fault in us that needs correction, we deceive ourselves. We will always make the frustrating mistake of confusing lust with love.

If you wish to find love and be free, hear the good news: the truth will set you free. God's plan for life and love is so profound that when we understand it, we will never look the same way at the relationship between a man and a woman. When we see God's plan for love, lust looks boring. When we see the truth about our bodies and sex, we change our lives but not out of guilt, or fear of pregnancy or disease. We change our lives because God's view of love is everything the human heart longs for. But it is not enough that we long to receive this kind of love, we must learn how to give it.

Therefore, let us offer our sexuality to God so that every action, word, glance, and desire will be lifted to him. Then he will guide our hearts toward the truth of human love. It is our turn for a sexual revolution, and those who lead our generation to victory will be those who have conquered lust by surrendering to the God of love. If we do not rise to this challenge to build a culture of life and a civilization of love, we have wasted that heroic enthusiasm, courage, and fortitude that our youth affords us.

It is my prayer that all who read this book will find guidance where there is uncertainty, encouragement where there is despair, healing where there are wounds, and a deep sense of the joy and peace that come from offering to God everything that we are, and everything that we do. As you read this, be assured that I have already been praying for you. Please keep all those to whom I speak about chastity, all those reading this book, and myself in your prayers as well.

> *"The Lord bless you and keep you: The Lord make his face to shine upon you, and be gracious to you: The Lord lift up his countenance upon you, and give you peace"* (Num. 6:24–26).

I

Chastity and the Meaning of Sex

1

Is chastity the same thing as abstinence?

Abstinence means that a person is not sexually active. If I heard that a guy was abstinent, that would not tell me much about him. Maybe he is a man with courage and character and is saving himself for his bride. Maybe he just can not find a date. Either way, abstinence is defined as what is *not* happening to a person's body —in other words, no sex.

Chastity is different because it is defined by what a person *is* doing with his or her sexuality. It means having the strength to use your sexuality according to God's plan, whether you are single or married. Living this virtue purifies your heart, heals your memories, strengthens your will, and glorifies God with your body. For an unmarried person it is sexuality dedicated to hope—saving sex for marriage. An unmarried person who has already had sex can still choose to be chaste by saving all future sex for marriage.

For the married and the unmarried it means having reverence for the gift of sex. Chastity is a virtue that defends love from selfishness and frees us from using others as objects. It makes us capable of authentic love. In short, abstinence ends in marriage but chastity holds marriage together.

2

Is chastity the same thing as virginity?

Some people think that chastity and virginity are synonymous but they are not. Not all chaste people are virgins, and not all virgins are chaste.

Because chastity means sexual purity, those who are sexually pure within marriage are chaste, even though they are not virgins. The same is true of unmarried people who have lost their virginity and pursue a life of purity. At the same time, it is possible to be impure, and therefore unchaste, even while retaining one's virginity. Many virgins assume, "As long as I retain my virginity, I am being good. Therefore, everything short of intercourse is okay." They may give parts of themselves to people they know they will never marry and assume that they are still pure because they are not having intercourse. Slowly they begin to believe that their body and sexual intimacy in general are no big deal. By the time they meet the person they truly deserve, they need a lot of healing for all they have given away.

But chastity is not something that can be lost forever because something shameful happened in your past. Virginity concerns our sexual history, but chastity is *not* concerned with the past. Chastity is a virtue that exists only in the present. There are plenty of people who have lost their virginity but are now incredible examples of purity. People often think that because they have lost their virginity, purity will always be out of their reach. It is not. Just as a person who has led a pure life can fall into immorality, a person who has sinned can return to purity. To be pure, it is necessary that your heart be directed to God. In his eyes, the repentant prostitute is purer than the lustful virgin. We need to remember that our worth lies in how God sees us, not in how others see us, or even in how we sometimes see ourselves.

3

Doesn't chastity ruin the spontaneity and excitement of romance?

It depends upon what you consider romantic. Passion is not the same as romance. Real romance is not what you find in a grocery store novel with Fabio on the cover. Giving in to one's hormones at the drop of a hat is not romance. This is lust, and while it may be spontaneous and temporarily exciting, using another person is not romantic. In fact, too many good romantic relationships have been ruined by lust.

Only humans are capable of romance because romance is when imagination and love meet. Sometimes a person's actions may appear romantic because they are so imaginative and thoughtful, but the actions may be done for the sake of seducing the other. This is not romance, because love is absent. Only when purity is present can one tell the difference between loving romance and selfish seduction.

In fact, romantic moments do not require physical intimacy —and the most romantic couples are the ones who realize this. They know that romance requires respect. You can have lust and passion without respect (as in prostitution), but you can not have romance without respect. When that loving respect for the other person is present, a man stirs up his romantic creativity not for the sake of getting something from a woman, but for the sake of expressing his love to her.

Lust, on the other hand, is boring because there is no room for mystery and anticipation. Everything secret is given away. The pure have more passion than the lustful, and it is precisely their passion that gives them the ability to build a greater kind of love. They exercise self-control not because of an absence of passion but because of the presence of love.

This is why there is something exciting in restraint, something that makes a chaste couple seem to glow in their wedding pictures. One woman in her mid-twenties pointed out that chastity "may be the proof of God, because it means that we have been designed in such a way that when we humans act like animals, without any restraint and without any rules, we just don't have as much fun." [7] In fact, people who misused their sexuality are longing for this kind of enduring love. They know that being loved is much more exciting than being used.

We need to remember that God is the author of romance. The Bible is his love story, and he is all in favor of human romances that reflect his love for humanity. For example, one of the most important ingredients for romance is thoughtful creativity. Psalm

139:17 says that the designs of the Lord are precious, and the book of Proverbs adds that God has glory in what he conceals.[8] Here is a story showing that fact:

I know of a married couple who returned from their honeymoon and sat down on the couch to look at the husband's old photo album. The album had pictures from a trip he and his family made to a church in Eastern Europe when he was a young boy. His wife was excited to see the pictures because she remembered visiting Europe as a child. As they flipped through the pages, she gasped when they came to a photo showing her husband sitting on the steps of the church with a crowd of people. She told him to look at the person sitting by his side in the picture. It was she. Sure enough, the two were sitting hip to hip. They did not meet at that time, but several years later God decided their paths would cross again. They fell in love, and you know the rest.

You have to wonder how often God intervenes like this in our lives. But when we distance ourselves from him, we sell ourselves short and settle for poor substitutes of the great love he wants to give us.

There is even more good news about the joys of chastity and romance, especially within marriage. The media tell us that the most exciting sex is outside marriage, but in reality the opposite is true. In 1999, *USA Today* published an article titled, "Aha! Call It the Revenge of the Church Ladies."[9] This report summarized the findings of the most "comprehensive and methodologically sound" sex survey ever conducted. The first three sentences of the report say it all:

> Sigmund Freud said they suffer from an "obsessional neurosis" accompanied by guilt, suppressed emotions and repressed sexuality. Former *Saturday Night Live* comedian Dana Carvey satirized them as uptight prudes who believe sex is downright dirty. But several major research studies show that church ladies (and the men who sleep with them) are among the most sexually satisfied people on the face of the Earth.

Now isn't that special?

The article concluded by saying that the Bible's teaching on sex would "come as a shock to those who believe that God is a cosmic killjoy when it comes to sexuality." The world constantly tells us that when it comes to sex, everyone is doing it, and the people having the most fun are the wild singles depicted on television sitcoms, while married life is dull and unromantic. However, according to widely-accepted research on the matter, "*The public image of sex in America bears virtually no relationship to the truth.*" [10]

Of those having sex, researchers found that the least satisfied were unmarried people. [11] Those who had sex outside of marriage were aware that while it felt good during the act, that did not mean they felt good about themselves afterwards. The guilt coupled with the anxious fear of being used, becoming pregnant, or contracting a disease lessened the sexual satisfaction of those who were promiscuous.

On the other hand, research showed that those who were married to a faithful partner had the highest reports of sexual enjoyment on both a physical and emotional level, and they were most likely to feel "satisfied," "loved," "thrilled," "wanted," and "taken care of." [12]

Contrary to what the world incessantly says, research shows that marriages benefit from a *lack* of premarital sexual experience. [13] In other words, great sex is not the result of sexual experience and technique. If anything, great sex is the fruit of a happy marriage, not the cause of it.

Physiological research has also shown that the human body is not designed for promiscuity. Dr. Winnifred Cutler is a leading authority in the biology of human reproduction and sexuality. She demonstrated that within a monogamous sexual relationship (marriage), the two bodies actually adapt to each other. The testosterone level in the man tends to reach its highest point at the same time that the estrogen peaks in his wife, creating even greater pleasure. This creates a kind of "hormonal symphony," that is impossible in passing promiscuous relationships. [14]

Lastly, it has also been discovered that "married couples who pray together are ninety percent more likely to report higher sat-

isfaction with their sex life than couples who do not pray together." [15] So if we are only interested in doing what gives the
most pleasure (which we should not be), the facts point back to
God's original plan: "A man leaves his father and his mother and
cleaves to his wife, and they become one flesh" (Gen. 2:24).

4

Isn't being chaste the same thing as being a prude?

The world looks at chastity and sees repression: a dull and frigid
lifestyle that is probably the result of fear or not being able to find
a date. "Those poor people living chaste lives. They do not have
a clue what they are missing. If only someone could liberate them
from their prudery." Sound familiar?

This may come as a surprise to those who think that chastity
and prudery are synonymous, but chastity has nothing to do with
having a negative idea of sex. In fact, only the pure of heart are
capable of seeing the depth and mystery of sex. For the person
who is pure, sex is an unspeakably wonderful gift and the body is
a temple of the Holy Spirit. Therefore, the foundation of chastity
is the dignity of every person and the greatness of sex.

Sure, chastity says no to sex before marriage. This is not because sex or the body is bad, but, on the contrary, because sex is a
holy mystery and a person's body is a holy temple. Holy things are
not open to all; they are only for those who meet the requirement,
who pass the test.

Think of the Holy of Holies in the Jewish temple, into which
no Israelite dared enter except the high priest once a year. The
doors were closed to other good and pious Jews not because the
Holy of Holies was unclean or disgusting or because the Jews
were embarrassed about it. On the contrary, it was restricted because it was so holy, so special, that it was appropriate only for
the one priest pledged to the temple's service to enter.

Our bodies likewise are holy and special, and access to this
temple is only for the one pledged forever to it in the sacrament

of matrimony. If we understood chastity for what it is, we would see that nothing testifies to the goodness of the body and sex as much as chastity does. Chastity affirms that we do not toy with sex precisely because of the greatness of sex. Those who treat sex as if it were a fair exchange for a nice dinner or six months of commitment are the ones who have yet to discover the greatness of sex. As writer Elisabeth Elliot said, "There is dullness, monotony, sheer boredom in all of life when virginity and purity are no longer protected and prized. By trying to grab fulfillment everywhere, we find it nowhere." [16] We constantly look for what we can get out of someone, how we can please ourselves and go with the flow.

This is why the impure are never satisfied or free. They have yet to learn that they can not be filled unless they empty themselves. Ironically, the satisfaction and freedom they yearn for is waiting for them in the place they least expect it—chastity. It trains us in self-control so that we can become truly free. "The alternative is clear," the *Catechism of the Catholic Church* tells us, "either man governs his passions and finds peace, or he lets himself be dominated by them and becomes unhappy." [17]

Chastity has a bad rap because it involves dying to ourselves. But we are not dying for the sake of death. In the words of Christ, "Unless a grain of wheat falls into the earth and dies, it remains alone; but if it dies, it bears much fruit" (John 12:24). The world sees chastity as death because it does not have the patience to see the life and love that spring forth from the sacrifice. It is not repression or guilt that motivates the chaste man or woman, it is the desire for real love.

The virtue of purity is wildly attractive. Freed from selfish sexual aggressiveness, the pure are empowered to love as we were created to love. Chastity is about having character. "I heard somebody say that you can judge your own character by the things you do in private," one young man said. "I'd take that a step further and say you can judge your own character by the things you do with your girlfriend." [18]

I travel around the country frequently to give talks about

chastity, and I often end up in conversations aboard airplanes about my line of work. Inevitably, people ask if I practice what I preach. After I explain that I am waiting for marriage before having sex, the person—without fail—looks bewildered. Then comes the universal question: "So . . . you just don't have the desires, then?" I have pondered all sorts of amusing ways to answer this, but the bottom line is that the world can not fathom a young person who has sexual desires and does not surrender to them. Working toward God's plan for love does not eliminate sexual desires, it orders them. The chaste person experiences sexual attractions in all their intensity but places love for the other above the temptation to lust.

Lust reduces men and women to the flesh, as illustrated in the song "Mambo Number 5." The lyrics read, "A little bit of Rita is all I need, a little bit of Tina is what I see, a little bit of Sandra in the sun, a little bit of Mary all night long, a little bit of Jessica here I am, a little bit of you makes me your man!" Why only a little bit? Because the singer is not man enough to handle an entire woman. Lust allows us to reduce others to "bits."

The problem with lust is not that lustful desires are too strong; they are too weak and lukewarm and self-absorbed. Prudery is fittingly represented as frigid but purity is white hot. Purity burns with a passionate love that puts lust in the freezer.

5

How do I know when I am ready to have sex?

The easiest way to know if you are ready to have sex is to look at your left hand. If you do not see a wedding ring, you are not ready for sex. This may seem like a simplistic answer, but look at the logic behind it. What does it mean to be *ready* for sex? Physiologically, we are able to have sex long before we are ready for it.

There are several reasons for this. First, sex can not be reduced to a biological act. Every aspect of the person is affected: the body, heart, mind, soul, and future. Just because your body is ready, it does not mean that you are ready. Second, sex has consequences that a twelve-year-old is not prepared to handle. One woman said,

> It took losing my virginity at a very young age, losing my self-respect and possibly my fertility, helping to ruin another person's marriage and family life, acquiring a non-curable virus, not getting the fulfillment that sex should provide in marriage, and living with the guilt that Satan always tries to make me feel . . . for me to realize how detrimental sex before marriage can really be.[19]

But instead of zeroing in on the negative consequences, it is more important for a person to understand what sex is. Then it becomes clear when we are "ready" to have sex.

We are commonly told with regard to sex, "Just say no." Why? "Because sex before marriage is bad." But we have never been told *why*—why sex *within* marriage is so good and beautiful and why this goodness and beauty is spoiled when we are not willing to wait for it. We need to hear the truth about sex and that we are worth waiting for. We need to accept the challenge to live out the demands of love. When we do this, and live according to the truth of our sexuality, we will make visible in our bodies the invisible reality of God—that he is love.

Once we are aware of the greatness of the gift of sex, we will have an attitude of humility toward it and only with God's permission will we lift the veil of its mystery. This demands faithfulness to him while we are waiting to find our spouse. And we can start preparing for a good marriage right now by avoiding anything that could harm a relationship with a future spouse.

If we do not understand the meaning of sex, we are likely to give it away to the first bidder. On the other hand, some people say that they want to save the gift of sex for the right person, someone they really love. But strong feelings of love do not make us ready for sex. This is clear in sexually active couples who are afraid of what sex means. They fear that their lovemaking could bring forth life. They also hide what they are doing from those who love them, such as their parents, and they fear that the incredible bond they have initiated might not be permanent.

You see, sex is saying wedding vows with your body instead of your voice. It is making a complete gift of yourself to another person. Consequently, it is obvious that premarital sex is dishonest —it is a lie in the language of the body. With your body, you are saying, "I give myself to you entirely. There is nothing more of me that I could give you," but in reality there is no such commitment and gift of self. There is a total physical gift but no total gift of the person. The gift is reduced to a loan or a lease because the body is given to the other temporarily. In short, you are ready to have sex when your body speaks the truth: "I am entirely yours. Forever." In other words, only in marriage can one be "ready" for sex.

6

Why is premarital sex bad? My friend just started high school, and she is trying to tell me that it is good and she is going to do it.

It might help to know that your friend is *not* on a quest for sex. Perhaps your friend has some hurt or loneliness in her life, and she figures that if she has sex, this will feel like love and security, and she will be happy. But if you look into her heart, you will see that she is not longing for a series of physical relationships with random guys. She is looking for enduring love and for intimacy, to be accepted by a man and cared for by him. She deserves these things, but she needs to be careful and courageous so that she does not fall for a counterfeit. There are plenty of boys out there who will tell her how beautiful her eyes are and how much they love her and will "always" be there. They will give her "love" for the sake of getting sex, and she may want to give them sex for the sake of feeling loved. Her heart is made for something better than this and she needs to realize that she is worth the wait. She cannot find happiness otherwise. As the Bible says, "She who is self-indulgent is dead even while she lives" (1 Tim. 5:6).

   The following are some of the bad effects of premarital sex; do not dwell on them any longer than is necessary to give her a reality check. What she needs more than the bad news about premarital sex is the good news about what she is worth and what plans God has in store for her. She needs to be encouraged to wait not because sex is bad, but because real love is so good. The negative consequences of premarital sex can be seen from the relational, physical, emotional, and spiritual points of view.

Consider how premarital sex can affect *relationships*. One study showed that the average high school relationship will last only twenty-one days once the couple has sex. Furthermore, *couples who sleep together before they are married have a divorce rate three times as high as couples who saved that gift for the wedding night.*[20] Couples who want what is best for their relationship or future marriage will wait. Beyond their own relationship, premarital sex frequently causes tension within families because of the dishonesty that usually accompanies the hidden intimacies. Relationships with friends are often strained and, when things turn sour, the gossip and social problems often become unbearable.

One high school girl wrote, "I am sixteen and have already lost my virginity. I truly regret that my first time was with a guy that I didn't care that much about. Since that first night, he expects sex on every date. When I don't feel like it, we end up in an argument. I don't think this guy is in love with me, and I know deep down that I am not in love with him either. This makes me feel cheap. I realize now that this is a very big step in a girl's life. After you have done it, things are never the same. It changes everything."[21] Another young person said, "I slept with many, many people trying to find love, to find self-worth. And the more people I slept with the less self-worth I had."[22]

Everyone talks about how hard it is to say no, but no one tells you how hard it is when you say yes.

In regard to the *physiological* side of things, it is dangerous for a young single woman to be sexually active. Because a teenage girl's reproductive system is still immature, she is much more susceptible to sexually transmitted diseases (STDs). In fact, early sexual activity is the number one risk factor for cervical cancer, and the second is multiple sex partners.[23] A girl's body, like her heart, is not designed to handle multiple sexual partners. Besides making herself vulnerable to STDs, your friend also needs to consider if she is ready to be a mother. Lastly, consider the fact that the rate of suicide attempts for sexually active girls aged twelve to sixteen is six times higher than the rate for virgins.[24] Tragically, these girls do not realize the purity and forgiveness that they can find in Christ.

New scientific studies also suggest that if a woman has multiple sexual partners, this will lower her levels of oxytocin that in turn will damage her ability to bond. Oxytocin is a neuro-peptide most commonly associated with pregnancy and breastfeeding. It seems to act as a human "superglue," helping a mother bond with her infant. It is also released during sexual arousal and there, too, seems to work as a "superglue." Since estrogen enhances the oxytocin response, females are capable of more intense bonding than males, and are more susceptible to the suffering that accompanies broken bonds.[25] According to an article by Dr. John Diggs and Dr. Eric Keroack, "People who have misused their sexual faculty and become bonded to multiple persons will diminish the power of oxytocin to maintain a permanent bond with an individual."[26]

In more basic terms, sharing the gift of sex is like putting a piece of tape on another person's arm. The first bond is strong and it hurts to remove it. Shift the tape to another person's arm and the bond will still work but it will be easier to remove. Each time this is done, part of each person remains with the tape. Soon it is easy to remove because the residue from the various arms interferes with the tape's ability to stick. The same is true in relationships, where previous sexual experiences interfere with the ability to bond.

But a sexual relationship that is properly bonded from the start, such as that between two virgins on their wedding night, has one advantage among many: Oxytocin helps to maintain the "high" of sex in a long-term relationship. This does not mean that if a person is not a virgin on the wedding night, he or she will be unable to bond with a spouse. It simply means that when we follow God's plan, we have the most abundant life possible.

The *emotional* side effects of premarital sex are also damaging to a young woman. It is not uncommon for a girl to have sex in order to make a guy like her more, or to encourage him to stay with her. She may compromise her standards because she is afraid of never being loved. Once he leaves her, though, an emotional divorce takes place. A person's heart is not made to be that close to a person and then separated. Since teenage sexual relationships rarely last, the girl's sense of self-worth is often damaged. Also, she sometimes concludes that if she looked better, he would have stayed longer. This mentality can lead to harmful practices, such as eating disorders like bulimia.

In her heart, a girl who has been used knows it. However, she may immediately jump into another sexual relationship to escape the hurt. If she tries to boost her self-esteem by giving guys what they want, then her self-worth often ends up depending upon those kinds of relationships. Her development as a woman is stunted because without chastity she does not know how to express affection, appreciation, or attraction for a guy without implying something sexual. She may even conclude that a guy does not love her unless he makes sexual advances toward her. She knows that sex exists without intimacy, but she may forget that intimacy can exist without sex. A girl on this track usually feels accepted initially but that acceptance lasts only as long as the physical pleasure.

Spiritually, sin cuts us off from God, and this is the most serious consequence of premarital sex. After going too far, many of us know all too well that cloud of guilt that weighs on our hearts. The solution is not to kill our conscience, but to follow it to freedom. It is calling us, not condemning us. Provided we repent, God will be there to welcome us home and let us start over (see John 8 and Luke 15).

What this all means is that our bodies, our hearts, our relationships, and our souls are not made for premarital sex. We are made for enduring love.

7

I heard that the Bible does not say anything about premarital sex. Is that right?

Anyone who says that the Bible is silent on premarital sex has not spent much time reading the Bible. The phrase *premarital sex* does not appear in the Bible, because Scripture uses the term *fornication* instead. This term is used in passages such as 1 Corinthians 6 where the apostle Paul says, "Do not be deceived; neither fornicators nor idolators nor adulterers . . . will inherit the kingdom of God. . . . The body, however, is not for immorality, but for the Lord, and the Lord is for the body. . . . Avoid immorality. Every other sin a person commits is outside the body, but the immoral person sins against his own body. Do you not know that your body is a temple of the Holy Spirit within you, whom you have from God, and that you are not your own. For you have been purchased at a price. Therefore glorify God in your body" (1 Cor. 6:9–10, 15, 18–20 NAB).

In 1 Thessalonians 4, Paul says, "For this is the will of God, your sanctification: that you abstain from immorality; that each one of you know how to control his own body in holiness and honor. . . . For God has not called us for uncleanness, but in holiness. Therefore whoever disregards this, disregards not man but God, who gives his Holy Spirit to you" (1 Thess. 4:3–5, 7–8). Elsewhere, the Bible exhorts us, "But fornication and all impurity . . . must not even be named among you, as is fitting among saints" (Eph. 5:3).[27]

This provides biblical support but it hardly answers the real issue. A person who claims that the Bible says nothing about premarital sex is often a person who is trying to suppress his conscience. Impurity is like cancer to our faith. When we live an immoral lifestyle and go to church, we have to grapple with the tension between how we are living and what we believe. If our behavior does not match our religious doctrine, one of them has to go.

As this tension mounts, we search for moral loopholes such as, "The Bible doesn't say it is wrong." When no loopholes are left, we grope for some reason to leave the faith altogether. "I think the faith is unreasonable," we argue. Or, "I don't care for organized religion." "I have doubts about the reliability of the biblical manuscripts." "I won't obey the Church because Church leaders don't always live up to its teachings." There is always something to divert us and keep us from studying and confronting the truth. We may claim to be "spiritual" but not "religious." The words of Paul are a challenge to us all: "They profess to know God, but they deny him by their deeds" (Titus 1:16). If we love God, we will obey him. If we do not obey him, we cannot claim to love him.[28]

People in this situation need to turn to Christ and allow themselves to be transformed. God's laws are not burdens. He is not a taskmaster who overwhelms us with rules so that we will blindly conform and live miserable lives to satisfy him. He wants to raise us up as his sons and daughters, training us in discipline so that we can become truly free to love. His laws exist because he loves us and wants us to share in that love.

"Jesus loves you." We hear that often but do we ever let the message sink in? Could it be that the God of love is not out to ruin our lives? Could it be that God has an interest in our love lives beyond making sure that we do not go too far? And could it be that he has established a Church to guide us into all truth by the power of the Holy Spirit? If we come to God with sincere and humble hearts, we will know the truth and be set free. We will not be bound by the illusion that God and his Church are out to rob us of our freedom.

8

Can't we accept that people have different values when it comes to sex? We need to be realistic—times have changed since the Bible was written.

A poll in Rhode Island recently asked students in grades six through nine if it is okay to force a young woman to have sex if the two of them have dated for six months or more. Two-thirds of the guys said that this was acceptable—and half of the girls did as well![29] Eighty-six percent of the guys said that it is okay to rape your wife, and twenty-four percent said that it was okay to rape a date if you spent "a lot of money" on her.[30]

Are you willing to "accept" those students' responses as those of "people having different values"? There is no doubt that times have changed since the Bible was written, but does the morality of an act depend upon where you live, when you live, or how many people agree with you? For example, if you jumped into a time machine, how far into the future would you need to go in order for child abuse to become moral? If you went back in time, took a poll of Nazi guards and the majority said that killing Jews was good, would that mean that we should be open-minded and accept their different values? Even today, if I were taken to court for shooting a clerk and shoplifting, do you think that the judge would be convinced of my innocence because I "just have different values"?

I hope you agree that no matter how times change, these acts will always be immoral. Why is it, then, that when we get to the sixth and ninth commandments (the ones regarding sexuality), people feel that morality is subjective and the Ten Commandments are multiple choice? Morality is objective, and a properly formed conscience can see this. No one likes to be told that what he wants to do is wrong, but we are not the authors of right and wrong. We need to overcome the temptation to judge God's laws by our standards, and begin measuring our standards by his laws.

We cannot construct our own private system of values. As Pope

John Paul II said during the 1993 World Youth Day in Denver, Colorado: "Do not give in to this widespread false morality! Do not stifle your conscience." Paul also warned us that "the time is coming when people will not endure sound teaching, but having itching ears they will accumulate for themselves teachers to suit their own likings, and will turn away from listening to the truth and wander into myths. As for you, always be steady, endure suffering, do the work of an evangelist, fulfil your ministry" (2 Tim. 4:3-5).

Modern culture tells us that if something feels good and we want it, we should have it. Go ahead. Gorge yourself. But when this mentality seeps into the minds of the youth, we get the moral anarchy expressed in the responses of the children in the poll mentioned above.

Although our civilization has lost the sense of sin, God still takes it seriously. Look at a crucifix. There on the cross is our answer. Sin is still sin and for this reason Christ's call to holiness applies for all times to every person on the globe. Christ makes demands on us precisely in the arena of sexual values. He asks much because he knows we can give much. We cannot dismiss our responsibilities by saying, "I gotta be me," or, "Boys will be boys." We will either glorify God or offend him by how we use the gift of our sexuality.

Ask yourself, "Do I *really* desire union with God?" If so, the quickest route is simple and humble honesty. Since God is truth, then our union with him depends on whether or not we are willing to submit our lives to the truth. We must love the truth and desire it with every fiber of our being regardless of how inconvenient it may be. In the words of Scripture, we must, "even to the death, fight for truth" (Sir. 4:28). This is the sincerity of heart that God longs to find in us.

One man noted, "There are few better tests for whether or not someone lives a life in submission to God than what he or she does with their sexuality. Sex is such a powerful and meaningful desire that to give it up and obey God in that area is a true sign of worship."[31] As Jesus said in his agony in the garden, "not my will, but thine, be done" (Luke 22:42). If we say that we love God but we still want to make up the rules when it comes to sexual desire, we have made pleasure our God. We should ask ourselves, "Do I love myself to the abandonment of God's will, or do I love God to the abandonment of my own will?"

9

What authority does the Church have to tell me not to have sex?

This question is really asking: "What authority does the Church have in my life at all?" Since some of God's commandments involve sex, and Christ ordered his Church to teach all that he commands (Matt. 28:20), the Church has the duty and authority to pass on to us what God has revealed about sexual morality. Scripture is clear that Jesus instituted his Church with such a mission. It would be unfaithful to Christ if it did not pursue this aspect of its mission.

Consider some of the ways Jesus made it clear that he was investing the Church with his authority. In commissioning individuals to go and preach his message, Jesus emphasized: "He who hears you hears me, and he who rejects you rejects me" (Luke 10:16). At the Last Supper, Jesus told the apostles that he was conferring a kingdom upon them (Luke 22:29). He previously had promised them that whatever they "bind on earth shall be bound in heaven, and whatever [they] loose on earth shall be loosed in heaven" (Matt. 18:18).

Jesus stated that the gates of hell would not prevail against this one Church (Matt. 16:18), which was to be the pillar and foundation of truth (1 Tim. 3:15). He invested the Church with his own teaching authority because he knew that he would not be with the apostles on earth forever. He established a Church with "bishops" who "give instruction in sound doctrine" (Titus 1:7, 9). The faithful are to submit to these spiritual leaders and defer to their authority in order not to be led away by strange and diverse teachings (Heb. 13:17). The authority of the apostles has been passed on to bishops from age to age through prayer accompanied by the imposition of hands (Deut. 34:9; 1 Tim. 4:14; 2 Tim. 1:6). We trace this "laying on of hands" in an unbroken line back to the apostles. The Holy Spirit guides the Church (John 16:13) so that it teaches what God entrusted to it. The Church guards its children as a mother watches over her young. The children may not always understand the mother's reasons for her rules, but they would do well to trust that her commands come from a loving heart and not a dictator's whims.

10

If premarital sex is so bad, why does it feel so good?

We can not determine the morality of an action based upon how good it feels. As a guy in his twenties, premarital sex would certainly be pleasurable to me. Rapists and child molesters feel pleasure, but no one would doubt that their actions are immoral. Likewise, things that cause tremendous pain can be acts of great love, as when one person gives his life for someone else. If we measured the goodness of an act by the pleasure received, then adulterers would be virtuous and war heroes would be scoundrels.

If you really want to know the morality of an act, "Do not conform yourself to this age, but be transformed by the renewal of your mind, that you may discern what is the will of God, what is good and pleasing and perfect" (Rom. 12:2, NAB).

11

If sex is good and natural, why shouldn't we have it whenever we want?

Just because a thing is good, it does not mean that it is without boundaries. For example, because sleep is good, imagine that you decide to sleep until one in the afternoon on a school day. You walk into school with the creases from your pillow still embedded in your face. When your teacher asks where you have been, you yawn, wipe the drool from your chin, and remind him that sleep is good and so you were enjoying sleep. You add that when you go home you will probably eat thirty pounds of Girl Scout cookies because eating is good, too. Needless to say, while sleep and food are good, they do have their limits. Similarly, the good gift of sex has its boundaries as well—and the boundary for sex is marriage. When we take sex outside of marriage, it is like taking fire out of the fireplace. The beautiful gift can quickly become destructive.

But what about the fact that sex feels so natural? Suppose that I am married and one day at work I decide to have an affair with my secretary. When I come home, my wife asks how my day was. I tell her that work went well, the drive home was pleasant, and that I cheated on her. Upon hearing this, she throws my belongings onto the front lawn. To ease her pain, I point out how "natural" the affair was. Needless to say, she would not be comforted. She is well aware that the fact that sex is natural is not a sufficient reason to engage in it.

Although pleasure is a natural result of sex, it is not the purpose of sex. In the same way, eating is naturally pleasurable but the purpose of eating is nourishment, not pleasure. If you confuse the primary reason for eating with its benefits, you become a glutton. Similarly, the purpose of sex is procreation and union (babies and bonding). If you confuse either of these purposes with the additional benefit of pleasure, you abandon love and use the other as an object of lust. Love is abandoned because using a person is the opposite of loving him.

When people argue that couples should be free to have sex outside of marriage, they do not realize what they are asking for. To "liberate" sex from the confines of marriage is like a child liberating his goldfish from its bowl—not a great idea. In the same way, the intimacy of sex was never meant to be separated from the total intimacy that makes up married life. It was not meant to be "free." By saying that sex should be given away freely, we are basically saying that it is not worth anything. When we divorce sex from marriage we will inevitably meet with disappointment. We are trying to grab the privileges of marriage without accepting the commitment and sacrifice that must accompany the gift of total intimacy.

12

Isn't it hard to say "no" all the time?

As I see it, there are two ways to live and to love. One sees temptations as obstacles to virtue, demanding a constant need to say "NO!" in order to obey all of God's seemingly burdensome laws. It is a life that is based upon "Thou shalt nots." Every day is an exhausting struggle to avoid offending God. If we live like that then it would be pretty hard saying "no" all the time.

Here is the alternative: Instead of living life trying not to offend God, live life trying to glorify him. Live each moment as an act of worship to God. Instead of seeing temptations of lust as obstacles to holiness, see overcoming them as the very means to holiness. Certainly this involves avoiding temptation and saying "no" to sin, but the motivation is the "yes" of true love.

As Mother Teresa said, "Intense love does not measure . . . it just gives."[32] Or in the words of Pope John Paul II, a young heart feels "a desire for greater generosity, more commitment, greater love. This desire for more is a characteristic of youth; a heart that is in love does not calculate, does not begrudge, it wants to give of itself without measure. . . ."[33] "There is no place for selfishness —and no place for fear! Do not be afraid, then, when love makes demands. Do not be afraid when love requires sacrifice. . . ."[34] "Real love is demanding. I would fail in my mission if I did not tell you so. Love demands a personal commitment to the will of God."[35]

So, the virtue of purity is not first a "no" to illicit sex, but a "yes" to authentic love. It is a "yes" to the truth of the goodness of our bodies and the gift of sex. It is not a prolonged series of "no"s but a continual "yes" to Jesus. Since we receive more grace each time we say yes to God, we soon see how possible and joyful this life really is. The Blessed Mother offers us the perfect example of how to live this when, in the Gospel of Luke, she gives us the recipe for holiness: "Let it be done to me according to your word" (Luke 1:38). The more we are able to imitate her "yes," the more joy and peace we will find in our lives. Someone asked Mother Teresa how we could become saints and she said: "Whenever Jesus asks something of you, say 'yes.'"

Living the virtue of chastity now means that you cherish your future marriage more than passing pleasures. Living with a pure heart will also prepare you to be a better wife or husband because you will learn how to express intimacy without always needing to be physical. It has been said that when a couple has healthy intimacy, the closer the two become the more they become themselves. When a couple is experiencing unhealthy intimacy, they usually feel as if they are losing their identity.

The "yes" I have spoken of is possible with God, because the love of God has been poured into our hearts by the Holy Spirit (Rom. 5:5). Tap into that and ask God for the grace to be pure. Have confidence, because with God's grace, *anyone* can achieve sexual purity. As you work toward the virtue of chastity, know that the desire to become pure is not something that comes from your body. There is no chastity gland located near your spleen, secreting abstinence hormones. Chastity arises from our will and is awakened and made possible by love. Granted, there will always be a tension between the desire to please God and the desire to act on our impulses. In the words of Christopher West, "Winning this battle takes faith in Christ, dedication, commitment, honesty with ourselves and others, and a willingness to make sacrifices and deny our own selfish desires. But love is not afraid of those things; love *is* those things."[36]

One practical note: Take a look at what surrounds you. If you constantly have to say "no" to various temptations, this implies that you end up in tempting situations on a regular basis. There will always be temptations, but we should work to avoid the occasion of sin. If you listen to music with sexually explicit lyrics, watch MTV and Jerry Springer, spend time in risqué chat room conversations, look through swimsuit or *Cosmopolitan* magazines and so forth, you are pouring lighter fluid on the fire that you are trying to extinguish. As the Bible says, "Who will pity a snake charmer bitten by a serpent, or any who go near wild beasts? So no one will pity a man who associates with a sinner and becomes involved in his sins. . . . Flee from sin as from a snake; for if you approach sin, it will bite you" (Sir. 12:13–14; 21:2). So, if there are bad influences in your life, replace them. Find better music and decent books to read. Also, increase your time in prayer, Scripture reading, and similar activities and you will be surprised how much easier it becomes.

13

How should I respond when people in my high school say, "Everyone is doing it"?

You could respond to this in any number of ways. For one, you could ask the person, "If I can prove that the majority of high school students are virgins, will you be abstinent?" The fact is, according to a 1997 survey, the majority of high school students are virgins. Between 1990 and 1997, sexual activity among high school guys dropped about 20 percent![37]

There are many "closet virgins" but the sexually active students tend to do a lot of talking. This gives the impression that "everyone is doing it," when in reality, the majority is not. The majority of high school students are virgins, and 71 percent of the teens who have had sex wish they had waited.[38]

You could also point out that the "everyone" who is "doing it" is also getting STDs, that "everyone" is breaking up three weeks after they have sex, and "everyone" ends up getting divorced if they stay together long enough to get married. You are in no rush to join any of these crowds. We all have a fear of not being accepted, or of being a loner if we do not conform to the world. But you must hold out for the higher standard of love.

The bottom line is this: What is our motivation? Is it to please God, or to conform to the world and make life-changing decisions based on the opinions of classmates, ninety-five percent of whom you will probably never see again after graduation? Stay strong. You are well worth the wait. Besides, the world needs to see young people who are not scared out of their minds to be chaste. This is something to be proud of, and if enough virgins on your campus realize this and have the courage to stand up, I would bet the saying "everyone is doing it" will soon refer to chastity.

2

Dating and Courtship

14

How do you know if you really love a girl?

What is love? I used to think of it as a warm, fuzzy feeling. When you see *her*, the world seems beautiful, the birds are singing, and everything reminds you of *her*. Your heart races whenever *she* walks into the room.

That is "being in love." This spontaneous emotional reaction is a lot of fun but we should not confuse these feelings with love itself. Some people think that they can tell how long a relationship will last based upon how powerful the feelings of attraction are. They spend massive amounts of time trying to decide whether or not they are in love.

What they are overlooking is that love is a decision to do what is best for another person, even if the warm fuzzies are long gone. But it is not enough to *want* to do what is good for the other. We must form our minds according to the truth that God has revealed so that we *know* what is good for the other, and we are not just doing whatever feels good. Once we know what is good for the other, all that remains is to follow through and live out that love in our actions.

Love does not "happen" to couples—it is something they *do*. It is a task. If the initial excitement of a relationship tapers off and we conclude from this that love is gone, we can be sure that love was never there to begin with. After all, if love is simply about having romantic feelings, how could a bride and groom promise each other that their marriage will last "until death do us part"? More likely, it would last until boredom do us part. Therefore, you can not determine the worth of a relationship by measuring the intensity of emotions.

Suppose you are married and your pregnant wife has food cravings. It is four in the morning and she wants you to go to the grocery store to get her fudge-brownie ice cream, pickle juice, and beef jerky. You roll over and look at your bride and she does not seem to be glowing like she did on your wedding day. At four in the morning, your world is not looking beautiful and the singing birds have gone mute. But after kissing her fevered forehead, you walk out the door and drive to the store. Has love gone away? Actually, it is more real than ever.

So, how do you know if you love a woman? Pope John Paul II has answered this question perfectly by saying that "*the greater the feeling of responsibility for the [beloved] the more true love there is.*" [39] The greatest example of this love is Christ. He alone perfectly reveals how to love a woman. If we ever need to know how to properly love a woman, all we need to do is look at a crucifix.

15

How do you know if a guy loves you or if he wants to use you?

If you ever want to know if a guy loves you, apply the love test. Here is how it works. I know a young woman who applied this love test on a first (and last) date with a particular guy. He made certain suggestions as to his intentions for the evening but she informed him that she practiced chastity. He responded, "That's okay. We can do other stuff" (implying everything short of intercourse). She proceeded to give him a crash course in the definition of chastity, and he responded, "So you mean that I'm not going to get *anything*?"

He sounded like an eight-year-old boy having a tantrum because his mother would not buy him a Lego set. His request coupled with the childish reaction shows that he had no idea what he was asking for. He assumed that buying her dinner should more than suffice to gain him access to the priceless treasure of her body. This is the blindness that comes with an irreverent attitude toward sex.

What this young woman did was not easy, but it was much easier than dating the guy for six months before realizing that he loved pleasure more than he loved her. Because she practiced the virtue of chastity, she saw through the manipulation that some people use to get others into bed. She knew that if a guy pressured her to give him her body, then he did not love her. Because of a woman's great dignity—she is made in the image and likeness of God—she deserves authentic love. She must never allow herself to be used or treated as a thing. Her body is priceless in the sight of God, and her heart is to be treasured.

Although this love test will weed out a lot of immature guys, only time will reveal a man's intentions. One man said, "If I sensed there was a moral dilemma in her mind, I would play any role necessary to reach the point where sex became inevitable."[40] There are many good guys out there but there are also plenty of predators who will tell a girl whatever she wants to hear. Therefore, a girl needs to proceed slowly, develop the skill of listening to her heart, and have the courage to follow it. Otherwise, a young woman may be left feeling as this fifteen-year-old did: "I felt strange, and in a sense, used. It was like we were both caring for the same person—him. I felt left out of it."[41]

16

I am a junior in high school and I have never had a girlfriend. Is that bad, and when should I begin dating?

This is not bad at all. In fact, it has some great advantages. Imagine that you started dating in the fifth grade and you had several relationships where you became very close to your girlfriends but then broke up. You gave part of yourself emotionally or physically to these random people. Later, when you meet the person you marry, you regret having kissed all those people and shared all those secrets. Although it did not seem like a big deal then, it sure adds up.

Do not worry that love will elude you if you do not rush into romance now. Take this time to be free from distractions, and ask yourself what God wants of you during these years. With all of your vigor and life, unreservedly give your youth to him. Try to outdo him in generosity, and watch what happens.

There is wisdom in taking your time before beginning a committed relationship. For example, only nine percent of people who started dating at the age of twelve will still be virgins when they graduate high school, whereas eighty percent of those who started dating at age sixteen will be virgins when they get their diploma.[42] This does not mean that if you started dating early, you will inevitably be sexually active in high school. I started dating in the fifth grade, which I now realize was pointless, and am still a virgin well into my twenties.

Taking your time will not only safeguard your virginity, it will also give you a better foundation for future relationships. For example, some people spend their entire high school years running around trying to find a date, frantic because everyone else seems to have one. Others always need to be dating someone new. As soon as one relationship ends, they jump into another because they feel incomplete without a date. They practically develop ulcers searching for their worth and their identity in relationships. Still others spend all four years staring into the eyes of a boyfriend or girlfriend. Their relationship consumes them, and by the time high school is over they are not sure of who they are or what their dreams are. The high school years are not meant for intense relationships that leave you feeling as if you would die without the other. This is a time to find out who you are, discover the world, and set the course for your life.

Nonetheless, it is not necessarily wrong to have a girlfriend in high school. Everyone wants the love of another person, but there is a season for everything. Right now, draw near to God so that you understand your worth in his eyes. Many people leap into relationships where their self-worth depends upon how the other treats them. Knowing what God thinks of you decreases your chances of falling into this trap.

So come to him, listen to his voice, and do whatever he tells you. As one woman said, "Inviting God to write the chapters of our love story involves work on our part—not just a scattered prayer here and there, not merely a feeble attempt to find some insight by flopping open the Bible every now and then. It is seeking him on a daily basis, putting him in first place at all times, discovering his heart." [43] He is the best guide when it comes to relationships, so stay close to him.

Lastly, your question presupposes that dating is the only option. It is not. Currently, there is a resurgence of young people leaving behind the modern concept of dating in favor of *courtship*.

17

What is the difference between dating and courtship?

The concept of dating is about eighty years old—as old as the automobile. Nowadays we are so used to it that we might not be able to imagine any other approach to relationships. But back before the car, the purpose of investing time with a young man or woman was to see if he or she was a potential marriage partner. The reason you expressed romantic interest was to woo the person toward that lifelong commitment. This process usually took place within the context of family activities. When the car was invented, this courting could be divorced from spending time with family because the couple could leave the family behind. Soon, the whole point of spending time together shifted from discernment of marriage to wooing for the sake of wooing. People would begin a relationship simply because they found the other to be cute and fun.

This put a new spin on the focus of relationships, and short-term relationships became commonplace. With this mentality, a person who dates successfully breaks up with everyone in his life except for one person (and this is supposed to be good preparation for a successful marriage). Of course, the majority of relationships do not end in marriage, but some become so intimate and intense that the couple might as well be married. If a breakup occurs, then they experience a sort of emotional divorce. It is not uncommon that by the time a person is married, he feels like he has already been through five divorces.

You may ask, "Well, what is the alternative? Am I supposed to shelter myself, put walls around my heart, and forget having a social life?" Not at all. The alternative is to rethink the way we approach relationships. Whether we admit it or not, the world has molded our views of preparing for marriage. We need to seriously ask ourselves: "What is the godly approach to relationships?" What would God have us do? Perhaps his ways are a 180-degree change from everything you have experienced. Perhaps you are burned out from the dating scene anyway, and could use a breath of fresh air.

Either way, I suggest a return to the principles of courtship. When I first heard of the resurgence of Christian courtship, I was skeptical. I remember thinking: "Oh, courtship. So if I want to spend time with a girl, I have to arrange for our families to go to a pumpkin patch together, followed by an exciting evening of board games, and then go home by seven. Woo hoo—real practical for a guy just out of college, living in Southern California." I had heard a great deal about courtship, but when I began reading books on the subject I ended up liking the idea more than I hoped I would. There was a great deal of wisdom that I had never tapped into.

Many books propose different forms of biblical dating, but the fact is that no one ever dated in the Bible. In some passages the parents arranged the marriage, and in other places we read of men going to foreign countries to capture their wives. The idea of traveling overseas and capturing a wife may have a certain appeal for some, but the Bible also provides guidelines that are more practical. Just because the concept of dating was unknown to those before the twentieth century, that does not mean that Scripture cannot help us understand the mind of God on the matter.

In Psalm 78:8 we read of a generation that had no firm purpose and their hearts were not fixed steadfastly on God. If that is a good description of our relationships, they need some reworking. We should be intent on finding out if it is the Lord's will for us to be with a certain person, and until we are ready to move in the direction of marriage, what is the point of committing to another?

Some may retort that this is all too serious, but should we be giving our hearts away to people who are in no position to make a real commitment? I am not proposing that you build an impenetrable wall around your heart, but that you guard it with prudence. We can wrestle over the terms "courtship" and "dating," but the essential thing is to glorify God and act wisely. The time spent prior to marriage must be a school of love where two young people learn the art of forgetting self for the good of the other.

While there is nothing wrong with becoming friends and spending time with members of the opposite sex, committed relationships should be entered into for the sake of discerning marriage. When we do enter into relationships, we should allow wisdom to chaperone romance. This involves having the humility to become accountable to others. Find a member of the same sex that you look up to, and go to him or her for guidance in your relationships. As Proverbs says, "Without counsel plans go wrong, but with many advisers they succeed" (Prov. 15:22).

There is also a great deal of wisdom in spending time together with the other person's family. Not only does it honor the parents, it also helps you get to know the family that you may one day join. Finally—and this may be a real eye-opener: How this person treats his or her family will likely be how he or she treats you when the feelings taper off. For example, if you are a young woman dating a guy who is disrespectful toward his mother and sisters, but is a perfect gentleman around you, guess what you have to look forward to if you settle down with him.

If we spend every waking hour tucked away in private gazing into our sweetheart's eyes, we will never find out who they are. The type of time a guy and girl spend together is essential if they wish to ground their relationship in reality. Spending time in service, with family, and even playing sports will help reveal who the person really is.

These are some of the principles of courtship: ask God's blessing at the beginning of a relationship; enter it with direction, toward discerning marriage; involve the families; be accountable to others; pace yourselves as you spend time together; and always listen for the Lord's guidance.

18

Where can I find a good guy? All the boys at school are interested in only one thing.

All women deserve a man who has one thing on his mind—doing God's will. Wait for a guy whose intention is to love you purely and lead you to God. Do not settle for less. You may be thinking, "Yeah, right. Where am I going to find a guy like that? I'll be in a nursing home by the time he shows up."

Put the matter in God's hands. Take this time to give yourself unreservedly to the Lord to build up his kingdom. Let him worry about building up yours. Too often people are so concerned with finding Mr. or Miss Right that they miss the opportunity to serve God in their singleness. Your job is to give your singleness to Christ. Keep your eyes on him instead of on potential future spouses.

I firmly believe that the strongest marriages are those in which both the man and the woman, prior to marriage, embraced the gift of singleness. Often, we never accept this gift because we are waiting for the gift of marriage, or exhausting ourselves maintaining passing relationships. Paul said, "I have learned, in whatever state I am, to be content" (Phil. 4:11). If a person does not learn to be content now, then when she is married, she may wish she were still single. After all, marriage does not change you internally; you are still the same person.

Besides, if a woman is happy and content in her present situa-

tion, she is more attractive. In fact, the ideal wife spoken of in the
Bible "laughs at the time to come" (Prov. 31:25). She anticipates
the future with joy, trusting in the goodness of God. Before we
can be happily married, we need to learn the art of being happily
single. That way, our happiness is not dependent upon outside
events, but upon an inner joy. In the words of Thérèse of Lisieux,
"The happier they are to be as he wills, the more perfect they
are." [44] I once asked a Missionary of Charity if she was happy in
the city where she had been assigned, thousands of miles from
home. She replied, "Anywhere. Wherever Jesus wants me to be,
that is where I'm happy." In the same way, learn to find your joy
by trusting in God. After marriage, you might never again have
the time to serve God without restrictions.

The best husband and father will be a guy who is single-hearted
for God. So be two of a kind. If you want a man of God, become a
godly woman. After all, men of virtue look for women of virtue.
Imagine all of the characteristics that you look for in a spouse—
that he be faithful, holy, respectful, loving, innocent, and so on—
and ask yourself, "Judging by the way I live, do I deserve a guy
like this?" Everyone makes mistakes but everyone is capable of
choosing to live a virtuous life.

As you grow in virtue, this will have a tremendous impact on
men. Many women become discouraged because of the kind of
guys they meet at school. But *the character of the men that a woman
attracts largely rests in her hands.* One woman said, "He will be as
much of a gentleman as she requires," [45] The fact is that the male
desire to please females is a basic one, and a woman who sets
high standards will attract young men willing to meet them. If a
young man wishes to enjoy a girl's presence, he will not be afraid
to be a gentleman. If a woman says that this is unrealistic, she will
continue to be frustrated and settle for less. If only young women
realized their power to help boys become men!

Set the standard high. Look for a guy who takes the initiative
to set wholesome guidelines for the relationship. Imagine if all
the young women in a high school or college decided to do this.
Sure, many of them might not have dates the next weekend, but it

would send a clear message to the boys that girls are serious about
being loved. Guys would soon be inspired to become worthy of
a woman.

In the meantime, pray for your future spouse and for discernment in your vocation. I once read about a fifteen-year-old girl
who felt she should pray for her future husband one random December night. When she met him some time later, she found out
that he was in a battle as she prayed, and nearly all of his fellow
soldiers were killed, while his life was spared.[46] God hears our
prayers.

So be at peace, and know that your heart's desires are God's
concern. The God who shaped the universe is infinitely concerned
with the small things. One day in Calcutta, a man who had a sick
daughter came to Mother Teresa. She did not have the specific
medicine that the child needed, since it had to be brought in from
outside India. As they were speaking, a man came with a basket
of medicine and right on top was the exact one the child needed.
Mother said, "If it had been inside, I would not have seen it. If
he had come before, I would not have seen it. But just at that
time, out of the millions and millions of children in the world,
God in his tenderness was concerned with this little child of the
slums of Calcutta enough to send, just at that time, that amount
of medicine to save that child."[47] So, know that your future is in
good hands.

19

Where, when, and how can I find the right girl for me?

Here is how many singles see the world of relationships: "God created earth—that's 199 million square miles, for the record. Then
God created my soul mate and put her out there somewhere. My
job is to find her, and God's job seems to be to hide her from me
for as long as physically possible. It is a delicate matter. If I sit at
the wrong table during lunch, or do not keep my eyes constantly
scanning, I might miss her. Destiny could slip from between my

fingertips because I was careless. I'm prepared to exhaust myself until I find her."

If this rings a bell, then it is time to hand the matter over to God. Search him out more zealously than you search for Miss Right. Do you think that if you remain single for a while to focus on God, he might let the woman he has planned for you slip by? Usually when we concentrate on serving the Lord, we give him a freer hand with us precisely because we are not getting in the way any more. I think that God waits on us sometimes, and that our tinkering and impatience can keep his plans from unfolding in their fullness.

Think: "If I am called to marriage, then God wants my future wife to have the best possible husband. But I can't become that man of God by moping around until God brings me Miss Right. If I will be a father one day, then I'll need to give my kids the gift of faith. But how will I do that if God does not first give me the gift of faith? And how can he give me that gift unless he purifies my faith through trials?" This is the time when he can give you that gift. This is where God wants you right now.

Mother Teresa used to say of acceptance,

> Every day we have to say yes. To be where he wants you to be. Total surrender: If he puts you in the street—if everything is taken from you and suddenly you find yourself in the street—to accept to be put in the street at that moment. . . . To accept whatever he gives and to give whatever he takes with a big smile. This is the surrender to God. To accept to be cut to pieces, and yet every piece to belong only to him. This is the surrender. To accept the people that come, the work that you happen to do. Today maybe you have a good meal and tomorrow maybe you have nothing. There is no water in the pump? All right. To accept, and to give whatever he takes. He takes your good name, he takes your health, yes. That's the surrender. And you are free then.[48]

So right now, embrace this season of singleness. Be there completely. Have you ever had a conversation with someone while your eyes were darting all over and your mind was somewhere else? A few years ago, I had a meeting with Fr. Michael Scanlan, my university's president. We spoke in his office for only twenty minutes, but I will never forget how present he was to me. He probably had a million other things to deal with, but he spoke to me as if I were the only person on earth. In the same way, we need to live entirely in the present moment, doing what we are doing, and being completely where we are. If God wanted us elsewhere right now, wouldn't we be there?

It is easy to waste our youth in making a future event or person the cause of our joy. There is nothing wrong with looking forward to marriage, but if anticipation and daydreaming consume us, we become our own worst tormentors, and we do little to build up the kingdom of God. We can become so preoccupied with regrets about the past and anxieties for the future that we never sit still to enjoy the peace Christ offers us today. We can easily become so concerned with finding Miss Right that we miss out on the joy of the single life.

Do not give in to feelings of despair, but draw near to God if this is a time of loneliness for you. Avoid self-pity. When you feel lonely, minister to those who are far lonelier than you. Ask yourself: How many homeless people do you know by name? More importantly, look for those who are hungry for love within your own home. By being sensitive to the needs of those under your own roof, you are training yourself to be a better husband.

So the first step in finding the right one is to *become* the right one. Become the man that God is calling you to be. Develop as a man of God by becoming a man of prayer. Do not wait for another person to complete you. Let God do that. Some guys think, "Since a wife is supposed to be your better half, I guess I'm only fifty percent complete until I find her. When I find her, she will fill my emptiness and take care of all of my emotional needs." If this guy finds a girl, it will not be a budding relationship—it will be a hostage situation.

We must be satisfied with being loved by God alone before we can truly love another. If you are in high school, realize that few people meet "Miss Right" during those years. You have plenty of time; there is no need to get into an intense relationship now.

Most people probably find their spouses in college, and do not get married until after graduation.

The second step is to go where the good young women are —at church youth groups, not at keg parties. Most importantly, seek God's kingdom first (Matt. 6:25–34). He is in charge, so be at peace because he knows well the plans he has in mind for you (Jer. 29:11–14).

20

I am a freshman in high school and am dating a guy who's five years older than I am. My mom does not like him, so we have had to see each other secretly. What should I do?

Ask yourself these questions: If you are having a secret relationship with a man who is willing to keep it hidden, what does this say of his character? It says that he is willing to be dishonest to get what he wants. If he is hiding a relationship *with* you, what makes you think he is not capable of hiding a relationship *from* you? Do you hope to marry a guy who is willing to hide a relationship? Beyond that, is there a reason he is not courting women his own age?

Also, examine how this relationship is forming you. To keep the relationship alive, you have probably lied to your family. But good relationships are founded on honesty with yourself, the other, your family, and God. To the extent that there is deception, there is an absence of love. The Lord has placed you within your family, under your parents' authority, for a reason. Do not let a guy come between you and them.

Whether we like it or not, moms have a lot of wisdom in this area—just like you will have a lot of wisdom when you become a mother. It takes maturity to realize that your parents may have valuable experience when it comes to relationships, and that they want what is best for you. Older people realize that the younger you are, the more an age gap matters in relationships. While no one would see anything wrong with a thirty-seven-year-old man

dating a thirty-one-year-old woman, it is more than a bit sketchy
for someone your age to be dating a fifth grader. In the high school
to college range, age is still a factor.

In fact, while this can be hard for young people to accept,
research shows that the place in the brain where reasoning and
judgment take place is not fully developed until a person reaches
his or her early twenties.[49] So there is a great deal of wisdom in
deferring to the guidance of people who are a bit older.

Though this may be tough to see right now, the situation is
setting you up for marital infidelity. Some of the excitement of
dating this guy is the fact that the relationship is risky and hidden.
Many guys and girls are in relationships like this and are unknowingly training themselves to be excited by what is forbidden. This
is harmful to marriages because once the couple is married, their
union is no longer forbidden or concealed. In order to have the
excitement they have grown to enjoy, the husband or wife may
turn to affairs.

Have the wisdom to step back and be honest with your family.
In the meantime, do not worry that you will never find another
guy who likes you. Think about whomever you had a crush on
four years ago and look at how your tastes have changed since
then. The same refining and clarifying of your interests will continue over the next several years.

Have confidence in love. If you sneak around, it shows a lack
of confidence in your love for each other, as if the success of your
love requires dishonesty. Have confidence in God as well. He can
take care of things. All he asks in the meantime is that you honor
your parents and wait to have the relationship until you are able
to be honest with them about it. You will not regret it. Meanwhile, remember: "Love is patient and kind; love is not jealous
or boastful; it is not arrogant or rude. Love does not insist on
its own way; it is not irritable or resentful; it does not rejoice at
wrong, but rejoices in the right. Love bears all things, believes
all things, hopes all things, endures all things. Love never ends"
(1 Cor. 13:4-8).

21

How come a guy will act interested in a girl, but after they sleep together he acts like he does not know her?

This kind of guy is not interested in guarding a girl's heart. His goal is sex and her goal is intimacy. He got what he wanted. The thrill of the chase is over and his respect for her is gone. She was only desirable as long as she was unattainable. Also, he might feel uneasy around her because he used her. When he did that, he missed the entire point of what it means to be a man. As a result, he might feel shame when he sees her; her face might remind him of his emptiness. He might also feel sad for her, so it is easier to ignore her. If a guy is exchanging the marital act with a woman before he marries her, he has made the mistake of asking for her heart before he is willing to hold and guard it with his life.

Here is a glimpse inside the heart of an honest guy who did just this:

> I finally got a girl into bed—actually it was in a car—when I was seventeen. I thought it was the hottest thing there was, but then she started saying that she loved me and was getting clingy. I figured out that there had probably been a dozen other guys before me who thought that they had 'conquered' her, but who were really just objects of her need for security. That realization took all the wind out of my sails. I could not respect someone who gave in as easily as she did. I was amazed to find that after four weeks of having sex as often as I wanted, I was tired of her. I didn't see any point in continuing the relationship. I finally dumped her, which made me feel even worse, because I could see that she was hurting. I felt pretty low.[50]

During premarital sex, two bodies are speaking a language of permanence that does not exist in reality. If either person's heart is invested in the union, that person will be disappointed, hurt, and angry when the breakup comes. One girl wrote, "I thought Mike really loved me, but last night we had sex for the first time and this morning he told my girlfriend that he didn't want to see me any more. I thought that giving Mike what he wanted would make him happy and he'd love me more."[51] To avoid this disappointment, a girl needs to realize that the marital act is the culmination and reward of total commitment, not a way to keep a guy interested.

Unfortunately, many young women think that a physical relationship will draw a guy closer. I have seen plenty of relationships that started out fine, but as the couple became more physical, the emotional, social, and spiritual aspects of the relationship atrophied. (*Atrophy* is what happens to a body part when it is not used. For example, the muscles of a paralyzed arm will wither away and become useless.) That is what happens to the other dimensions of a relationship when physical intimacy dominates. The solution is restraint. A young woman will find the intimacy for which she yearns only by respecting herself.

22

I am sort of seeing this guy but he is still unsure of his feelings because he likes another girl, too. Even though we agreed that we would not date other people, I found out that he was dating this other girl and even kissed her. Yet he wants to keep the door open in our relationship. What do I do?

I once read about a husband who was cheating on his wife. She was afraid of losing him so she allowed the affair to continue. This caused the husband to lose any respect for her and he ended up inviting the other woman over to their house. His wife even allowed her to sleep in their bedroom! This is what can happen when a woman does not demand the respect and commitment that she deserves. She becomes her own worst enemy and men treat her badly because she lets them. This woman should have told her husband: "I know what's going on, and you must make a decision. Choose between her and me. If you choose her, it will hurt me but I will go on and I will be okay. Regardless, I will not sit here while you flounder around in indecision. If you can't commit to me, I'll take that as a goodbye."

I encourage you to have the same clarity with this guy. Never allow a partner in a relationship to simply break a commitment. If he wanted to see other people, he should have had the guts to come to you and say so rather than sneaking around after he said he was going to date you exclusively.

On the other hand, if he had not committed to seeing you exclusively then he was not being dishonest or breaking a commitment in seeing someone else. You may not like what he did, but that is one of the things that happens when you "sort of" see someone. Those who do not want such things to happen need to have the guts to say, "I don't think we should date other people" and find out if the other person agrees.

Delaying this too long can set people up for problems. You hear of couples who say, "We're not boyfriend and girlfriend but we are seeing each other," or "We aren't dating but he told my friend that we are a thing." Once you have built emotional ties with someone, do not settle for a relationship that is just a "thing." A thing is something that grows out of the side of your foot. You deserve clarity when it comes to commitment. Girls who never learn to expect it often end up with a cohabiting boyfriend who, instead of proposing to her, gives her a "promise ring" because he is too scared to commit. She is flattered and pacified because any sign of commitment from him is exciting for her.

You had an exclusive relationship with your boyfriend and he violated it. Great relationships do not "happen." They are the result of a conscious decision to respect yourself. You need to learn this respect for yourself so that you do not constantly end up with guys who refuse to respect you. In the situation you are in now, this guy only deserves to see you on a "more than friends basis" if he has clearly ended the relationship with this other girl and intends to be with you exclusively.

Even if he does, I would not necessarily jump back into a relationship with him. He needs to see that you are not waiting on him hand and foot, instantly available should he become tired of dating someone else. Take your time and do not exhaust your-self by clinging to him. Also, do not expect an overnight charac-ter change in him, no matter how eloquently he speaks about a change in his heart.

Trust takes a long time to build, and if he expects you to trust him with your heart, there is a great deal of rebuilding that needs to happen. Since he has already broken a commitment to you once, there is no guarantee that this will not happen again. Sometimes a girl will like a guy so much and will be so insecure that she is willing to overlook his deception and unfaithfulness as minor glitches in the relationship. He will say that he is sorry and he loves her, and she lets him right back to hurt her again. Do not make this mistake. Honesty is one of the most important elements in a good relationship. In the words of one doctor, "to the extent that you are being deceived, there is no relationship."[52]

Also, if he has just ended a relationship, you do not want to get him on the rebound. Further, take a good look at why he is breaking up with this other girl. This says volumes about a person. Some people jump from one relationship to the other according to how strong the feelings are. When they are weak, they jump ship; when they are strong, they jump aboard. They think that once the feelings are gone, love is gone. It turns out that they love the feelings of being "in love" more than they love the actual person.

23

This girl that I like is dating a guy who is a jerk to her. We're only friends but sometimes I feel guilty for liking her, since she is taken. But I wonder if the feelings are from God because they will not go away. What do you think?

Usually we are not responsible for feelings of attraction, even re-curring ones. What matters most, though, is not how you feel toward this girl but how you should act toward her. As long as she is committed to another guy, even if you think he is a jerk, you must not encourage her to violate this commitment behind the other guy's back. You could let her know—within the bounds of charity, of course—that you think she deserves someone better than the guy she is with. (Assuming that your opinion of the other guy is a fair one, not based on resentment or envy.)

Of course, unless you think her likely to be receptive to this message, such a move might be unwise, but that is a question of prudence, not of morality. If she seems happy in her current relationship, she could very well take offense at such a suggestion. In that case, it might be wiser simply to remain on friendly terms with her and see how things turn out. Love her as Christ would, and hope that from this, she will realize that she deserves someone better than her current boyfriend.

As far as feelings "coming from God," you must not assume that an attraction to another person means that this is someone God wants you to marry. God designed us to be attracted to what is beautiful and so we experience attraction when we see beauty. That does not mean he intends that we pursue each beautiful person we see. For example, even in marriage there may be times when you experience feelings of attraction toward women other than your wife. Needless to say, this attraction is not God's way of saying that you should leave your wife. As for now, live with the peace of knowing that God's plans for you are perfect. Always say yes to him, and you will never miss out.

24

If you met a girl in her mid-twenties who was still a virgin, what would you think, really? Would you think that something was wrong with her? Wouldn't that scare you off?

Speaking as someone who is in his mid-twenties, let me say this: Nothing adorns a woman with as much beauty as does purity! Nothing is more attractive than holiness. Anyone can recognize this. I once heard of a group of young men who called themselves the "Spur Posse." They competed to sleep with as many women as possible, but every one of them admitted that he wanted to marry a virgin. They all recognized that virginity was a priceless treasure. Unfortunately, they thought it was okay to sleep with the future brides of other men, even though they did not want anyone to touch the women they would marry.

In the book *When God Writes Your Love Story*, Leslie Ludy reported a conversation that she overheard. Four men were speaking about what they looked for in a woman: " 'A woman who has mystery—who guards her heart and isn't easy to get.' 'A woman who has backbone. High standards.' 'A woman who is focused on God and isn't easily distracted by men.' 'A woman who doesn't throw herself at me, but allows me to win her heart over time.' " Leslie asked the men what their opinion was of girls who were easy. They all said, " 'It's disgusting.' 'A real turn off.' 'Totally unattractive.' " Leslie asked one more question, " 'How do you feel about a girl who is careful about guarding her emotions?' 'I have the utmost respect for a girl like that.' 'That's the kind of girl I want to marry.' 'If I'm interested in a girl, it may be frustrating if she doesn't fall for me right away, but deep down I am all the more intrigued by the challenge of winning her heart.' " [53]

If I were to meet a woman who was still a virgin (and there are plenty my age), I would not think that something is wrong with her. I would think that something is right with her. I would think, "Here is a woman who is willing to sacrifice for the sake of love. Here is a woman who knows the respect she deserves. Here is a woman who knows full well that her body is a temple of the Holy Spirit. Here is a woman."

Since virginity can only be given once, do not lose it. You lose keys and cell phones but your virginity is not meant to be lost, as if you had misplaced it somewhere. *Give* your virginity once and for all to the one true love of your life—your spouse—and to no other. This will be a tremendous blessing to your marriage. In fact, a recent survey of thousands of women revealed that non-virgin brides increase their odds of divorce by sixty percent. [54]

There is *nothing* wrong with you if you cherish the treasure of your virginity. Do you want to explain to your future spouse that you gave away your virginity in order to prove that you were normal or popular? Imagine the joy of being able to tell your groom that the gift of your body belongs entirely to him, and to no other. Now imagine if you were not able to tell him that. You have saved it this long because you know its value and you simply need a reminder that you are on track. You are.

The world talks so often about having "sexual experience" and being able to "perform" that it is no wonder no one seems satisfied. All the talk leaves people afraid to be inexperienced. But why? The marital act has nothing to do with performing. I do not know about you, but I have no plans to have a panel of judges with numbered cards sitting in my honeymoon suite. Do not worry about not having enough experience. You will have your entire married life to figure it out.

So, virginity does not scare me off. Purity before marriage is beautiful and helps unite the couple for life. I have received several e-mails from husbands who are having difficulty in marriage because their wives have been with other men before them. The gift of a pure body, a pure mind, and a pure heart is the greatest gift you could ever give your spouse. After all, the value of a gift increases immeasurably if it exists only for the one to whom it will be given. Anyone who thinks that having more sexual experience makes the gift of oneself better is like someone who thinks that if you chew your gum before you give it to someone he will be more impressed by the gift. Prepare to give your future spouse the best gift you possibly can, and the Lord will bless you abundantly.

25

I have decided to save sex for marriage, but I am unsure about being completely chaste with my boyfriend. Any advice?

I am glad you recognize that chastity is more than abstinence from intercourse, but there is a lot of wisdom in saving sexual arousal for marriage as well. The reason you hesitate to take this next step is that the connection between chastity and true love may still be hazy for you. Let's take a look at the link between the two.

We all desire love, but in the words of Pope John Paul II, "*Only the chaste man and the chaste woman are capable of true love.*"[55] He also said that *purity is a requirement of love.*[56] Why is this?

I think we can agree that it is easy to mistake physical intimacy for love. This is understandable since physical intimacy has such a unifying power, which is an attribute of love. The problem is that lust also has a tendency to draw two people together. It is a counterfeit oneness that may be hard to distinguish from the real thing, especially if we have never known healthy intimacy before. The physical closeness seems to meet deep needs that are not filled elsewhere.

We all have a need to be loved, but some people stay in unhealthy relationships because it seems to bury the hurt and loneliness. This is where chastity comes in because it alone has the power to differentiate between love and lust. For those who seek love, chastity is the answer.

Have you ever had a crush on someone and formed an idealized image of him, only to see a different person emerge when your emotions faded and reality set in? Was it the other person who changed or was it you? He probably did not change at all. You just opened your eyes. Just as having a crush on a person clouds our objectivity, physical intimacy does the same. Personally, the more physical my relationships have been, the more difficult it was to judge their worth while I was in them. After a relationship ended, it was easier to evaluate how healthy the relationship was. But while I was in it—and to the extent that we were physically involved—the tougher it was to recognize that it was not worth keeping. Frequently, we do not want to look at a relationship objectively because we do not want to admit that it is not love. We do not want to lose the other person.

Whenever love is present, there is a desire to please the other. This is especially common in young women who want to please guys in order to win their affection. However, love sometimes demands that we refuse to please the other, because what the other finds to be pleasing is not what is best for him. You would agree that when you refuse to have sex with a guy, it does not mean that you do not love him. It just means that you love him more than he may be able to understand. If we act out of a desire to please, then we are not really being loving to the other person. We are not doing what is best for him.

Sometimes, people who are intimate in ways short of sex stay together for a time. Usually, however, this becomes old and the couple pushes back the boundaries trying to find new levels of excitement and closeness. Before long, all that is left is sexual intercourse. The couple depends on physical pleasure to feel close to one another since they do not know how to express love in other ways. In the long run, the couple's impatience for sexual oneness tends to end up causing their separation. They have deprived themselves of the opportunity to grow in love, and thus to experience true joy.

Don't feel you will miss out if you live chastity to the fullest. Sure, you will experience an initial loss of the physical union that you desire, but you move beyond this when you see the value of the other person and the benefits of a chaste lifestyle. In the end, the only thing you miss out on is the empty counterfeits of love. While chastity is not the easiest choice, it is the best one.

To see how this works on a practical level, consider your options. A guy who does not intend to save sexual arousal for marriage will often approach a date as a formality to get through before the real "fun" can start. When a couple is striving for purity, then the dates can actually be enjoyed as time spent getting to know each other. You are free to fall in love for all the right reasons. If you do not embrace chastity but still wish to remain a virgin, where does this leave you? You will become all revved up, only to repeatedly slam on the brakes. Not only is this unloving because it arouses desires that you can not satisfy morally, it also leads to sexual frustration.

Often, a couple will share the gift of sexual arousal to feel closer, but they end up feeling alienated from each other and regretful. They would be much closer if they entrusted the relationship to

God, and made sacrifices together to glorify him. Love always involves struggle, so if they are both willing to be generous with God, this will create a union between their hearts that no illicit pleasure can match. Purity will become their superglue.

One man told me that the power of temptation rests on the deceptive promise that sin will bring more satisfaction than living for God. It is only God's way that can satisfy us. In the words of Psalm 16:11, "Thou dost show me the path of life; in thy presence there is fullness of joy, in thy right hand are pleasures for evermore." We all desire happiness, but sin and happiness cannot live together. Sin is a counterfeit of happiness that brings with it the ugly companions of shame and regret. Sacrificial love brings true joy, and a life of virtue brings happiness. Try it and see. Where there is no chastity, there is selfishness. Where there is selfishness, there is no love. Where there is no love, there is no joy or peace. No wonder Pope John Paul II said, "Chastity is the sure way to happiness." [57]

26

Sometimes my boyfriend respects my wishes but sometimes he pressures me to do stuff that makes me uncomfortable. I do not want to lose him, so what should I do? I made some big mistakes in past relationships.

I understand your fear of confronting your boyfriend, but the bottom line is that you must risk losing him. Every human being was created to be loved and never to be used. But if you are even slightly afraid that he will lose interest in you when you end physical intimacies, ask yourself: Is he interested in you, or in pleasure? Deep in your heart, I think you are afraid that he may be in this for the physical relationship. You have been used before and your greatest fear is that you will be used again.

There are two options open to you. One is to give in to whatever he wants (which is no guarantee that he will stay). The other is to follow your heart. Look into your heart to discover why you do not feel comfortable doing these things with him. It is probably because the acts degrade you. You deserve better, but suppose that you were willing to give your boyfriend whatever he wanted, for fear of losing him. Would his respect for you go up or down? Down. If you stand firm and show that you will not compromise your values, then he will respect you more—even if he leaves you because he is in search of a girl who does not know what she is worth. You must take this risk if you want love.

A young woman may abandon her morals because she likes the fact that a boy desires her so much. She may be starving for love and willing to settle for lust. But what usually happens is that the guy loses respect for the girl, becomes bored, and leaves. Other times, he sticks around as long as she is willing to satisfy his desires. I have heard of many young women who say they do certain things with their boyfriends because they thought that the guys would like them more. One girl wrote, "He had convinced me that what we were doing was okay, and so that is what we did. The whole time I felt I was doing something wrong, but I silenced myself for the good of him. Little did I know the effect this would have on me. It was as though someone had slowly scooped away at my soul and let it deteriorate."

You know in your heart that this kind of relationship is not what you are looking for. Another young woman shared:

> I had been told all my life that sex before marriage was wrong, but no one ever told me why. In the twelfth grade I found myself dating one boy for a long period of time. We spent a lot of time alone and as a result our relationship became more physical. I felt guilty, bitter, frustrated, and dirty. Because of those feelings, I would say to him, "We need to stop having sex, or at least slow down." Well, we tried to slow down, but that didn't work. Instead of getting closer, we grew farther apart. After two years of dating I finally said, "No more sex," and he said, "Goodbye." Since then, whenever I dated another person for a length of time, sex became a part of the relationship. Tears always came because I knew I had blown it again. [58]

If your boyfriend loves you, he will not pressure you to do things you are uncomfortable with. Suppose you say, "I don't feel comfortable doing that with you." If he responds, "Why not? You used to do it," or "What's your problem? Come on, I love you, this will make us so much closer," then he is not respecting you. Often, a guy will insinuate that he really loves you but he may need to leave if his desires go unsatisfied. This is definitely not love."Love waits to give, but lust can't wait to get." [59]

Ask yourself this question: "When it comes to my body, will my boyfriend take everything that I'm willing to give him?" If this is the case, then he is not concerned about your soul. His goal is pleasure. While it may temporarily feel like love, you know in your heart that it is not. For example, consider what a guy named Jordan said in an article in *Complete Woman* magazine: "Sex is extremely important to me. In fact, once I felt compelled to break up with a woman I really loved because we didn't have enough sex. . . . The lack of sex nearly killed me." [60] (Apparently he was rushed to the hospital for lack of sex.) Anyway, if this is how Jordan treats women he "really loves," it is hard to imagine how he treats other women.

Pray for courage and wisdom, and let your boyfriend know that you want to be pure from now on. Good relationships require good communication. You need to be open with your boyfriend about what is on your heart. You deserve a guy who will not only allow you to become pure, but will also lead you to purity. Sometimes a guy will reply to the love test by saying, "No more sexual stuff? That's okay—I love you unconditionally." The girl melts but his behavior gradually returns to the way it was before. In these cases, a girl needs to persevere in purity and see what happens. If he sticks with you as you grow in holiness, and he brings you closer to God by his actions, then the sacrifices you have made together will be good training for marriage.

As for now, the best thing you can do for him is to grow in holiness yourself. It will inspire him to become worthy of you. When women are pure, they become "possessors of a deep and wondrous secret that is revealed only to the one who proves himself deserving of her." [61] This sense of independence in a girl appeals to guys. If women easily give themselves away, they should not be surprised to find themselves in a culture of men who feel no need to commit to them.

But is this guy the one for you? To be honest, I do not think so. I think you may know that and be afraid of starting over. Or perhaps you want to make this work out, so that you do not have to address the hurt. But it will be much better in the long run if you take a hard look at your situation now. One reason I doubt the strength of this relationship is because you said that "*sometimes* he will respect my wishes.*" This is a big warning sign, suggesting that the rest of the time he is placing his hormones on a more important level than you as a person. That says a great deal about his character. Any guy can say yes to sex. But how many can say no? If he can not say no to temptations now, how will he say no when temptations come in marriage?

27

There is a guy that I really like, but I am not sure if he is interested in me. I want to find out if he is, but I do not want to scare him off. Should I call and tell him, or should I play hard to get?

Possibly neither. First of all, playing games is never a good idea. A girl who is real is much more attractive than a girl who wants to play mind games. After all, if you play games to make guys like you, then when do you stop playing? If you play hard-to-get to win a guy, then you may feel the need to maintain that teasing behavior to keep him interested. A mature relationship needs to develop without having to rely on games.

If you need to pretend to be someone you are not in order to win another's heart, then what will happen in the long run? The entire relationship will be built on deception. This is the opposite of love, which "rejoices in the truth" (1 Cor. 13:6, NAB). Love is patient, and it trusts that God knows what he is about. There is no need to take the situation into your own hands so that you can make things happen at your own pace. God's pace is much better.

But calling him up and telling him openly how you feel may not be a good idea either—unless the two of you already have a strong personal friendship. To begin with, there should be a season of friendship before you rush into a romantic relationship. Failing to cultivate this could be harmful in the long run, since these things need time to build. Imagine a girl building a dollhouse. She is in such a rush to play with the finished product that she glues the house together in thirty minutes, and moves all the furniture in. She ignores the directions to wait a day for the glue to dry before even touching the house. Naturally, it collapses. Similarly, you must establish a foundation and give the friendship time to develop.

Without this foundation of friendship, revealing your feelings for him too soon could hinder mutual feelings from developing in his heart. When those feeling do take root in him, they will show in due time. Until then, work on building a graced friendship. If he does reciprocate, then you will again be called to be patient. A lot of people become "more than friends" without spending much time *being* friends—which often ends up meaning they are really *less* than friends.

28

My boyfriend has a lot of problems. I am scared of him sometimes and my friends say that he is bad news. We have been pretty physical, but I want to stay in the relationship to help him. What should I do?

The purpose of dating is to find a worthy spouse, not to rehabilitate a troubled guy. It sounds like you need to step back from this relationship. Many young women with good hearts want to play the role of heroine for a guy who has a rough life, but they end up wounded and the guy is not much better off. A girl might stay in the relationship because she does not want to hurt the guy by leaving. But it will harm the guy (and her) more if she does not take a step back. Until he can deal with his problems in a way that is not destructive to him or to others, he is not ready to be in an intimate relationship. Friendship? Maybe. Dating relationship? Not now.

According to God's word, "A man of great wrath will pay the penalty; for if you deliver him, you will only have to do it again" (Prov. 19:19). It is not your job to save this guy from all of his problems. Let him know that you are there for him, but that you need space for yourself. This is not selfishness. It shows a healthy respect for yourself, and that is the foundation for any good future relationship.

If he tries to lay a guilt trip on you or intimidate you, it is all the more evidence that you need to back away. If he hurts you, then the sooner this ends the better. On the opposite side of the coin, do not use physical pleasure to cover up the pain of the relationship. Instead, listen to your friends. They are there to look out for you, and I do not think that you will regret following their advice.

A recent study showed that when it comes to predicting the success or failure of a relationship, no one knows better than the friends of the girl. Not the couple themselves, not the guy's friends, but the girl's friends are the most reliable judges of how strong a relationship is and how long it will last. [62] As Proverbs 27:6 says, "Faithful are the wounds of a friend." This means that although their advice may be painful to receive, it will be best in the long run to follow it.

As difficult as it may seem to walk away, it will only be more difficult later to patch up the hurt that has been caused by staying in the relationship too long. Two factors should influence this decision: You are worth more, and he needs this space. If you do not understand your value in God's eyes, then it is easy to seek your worth in relationships, even unhealthy ones. Even an unhealthy relationship makes you feel desired, and so you settle for it.

Right now, while he is still single, the most loving thing you can do is to show him that he cannot deal with his hurt by hurting others. He needs to know that his behavior is unacceptable. Using a little child psychology may be helpful here. According to Drs. Cloud and Townsend in their book *Boundaries with Kids*, "Setting boundaries without setting consequences is a form of nagging. The disrespecter learns that his greatest problem is not the hurtfulness of his behavior, but only the annoyance of your complaining."[63] As long as you stay in the relationship and take the abuse, it sends him the message that his behavior is fine. You deserve better. Imagine what it would be like to be cherished by a man who protected your purity.

29

My friend is in high school and she is always getting into bad relationships with college guys who do not respect her. Now a guy wants her to leave her mom and third stepfather, and move in with him. What can I do?

As you realize, your friend really needs to take a break. Because she comes from a broken family, she may have a void in her life that should have been filled by the love of her father. It is common for a young woman who did not receive her father's love to jump into the arms of older guys to receive the missing affection, attention, and acceptance. One woman said, "I thought about the girl who this very night will lose her virginity because she is searching for her daddy's love. And I want to be able to stop her somehow and tell her that she will never find it in another man."[64]

Your friend might fear abandonment and may confuse the physical affection of boys with love. If she had a loving father who protected her and sacrificed for her good, then she would be more likely to wait for such a man to come into her life. Since she never received this gift, she does not know how a man should properly treat a woman.

There may also be a deep connection between the absence of her father in her life and her willingness to live with disrespect. Sometimes when a child had a distant or critical parent, the child may want to please people who hurt her in order to receive their love. In trying to mend those original wounds, the child will put up with just about any form of disrespect. These are deep problems, and living together with a boyfriend will not solve them.

In fact, living together with this guy is one of the worst things she could do. See the resource section of this book for a web site on cohabitation that shows the consequences of living together. Perhaps you can show your friend some of the facts in order to discourage her from moving in with him. She deserves a loving and lasting relationship, and if she truly wants this, then she needs to work toward it and start making smart decisions for herself and her future.

There is a web site listed in the Resource section that can provide some valuable pointers that can help you see what a healthy relationship looks like. She does not know what to expect from a man, so she will take what she is given. This is why she needs space to figure out who she is and what she really wants.

30

How do you know if you should break up with the guy you are dating?

Ask yourself the following questions (the more questions you answer with "no," the more reason you have to break things off): Has my relationship with him brought me closer to God? Can I see myself marrying him? Would I like my children to grow up to be just like him? Am I dating to discern marriage? Do my parents approve of him? Is he one-hundred percent faithful? Do I feel safe, honored, and respected around him? Is he clean of any drug, alcohol, or pornography problems? Has this relationship helped me to become the woman I hope to be? Does he bring out the best in me? Does he respect my purity? Does he love God more than he loves pleasure? Can I honestly say that the relationship is emotionally, physically, spiritually, and psychologically healthy? Has the relationship brought me closer to my family and other friends?

Ideally, you should be able to announce an emphatic "YES!" to all of the above questions. The more negative answers you have, the more reason you have to think twice about the relationship.

St. Paul tells us that an unmarried woman is anxious about the things of the Lord, about how she can serve him and be holy (1 Cor. 7). Are you free to be anxious about the things of the Lord or are you consumed by emotional conflicts with your boyfriend or consumed by your relationship in general? Some young women are willing to stay in bad relationships so that they never have to be alone. They will put up with disrespectful behavior, compromise their values, and stay in a dead-end relationship that should have ended long ago. Many couples become so close that they feel as if the other person is their entire world. If they let the person go, they fear that they will have nothing left and love will be lost forever. Do not give in to this fear.

If he has some major issues, do not move toward marriage expecting that these issues will resolve themselves over time. This is denial. If he treats you disrespectfully, lovingly confront his behavior. If he listens, apologizes, accepts responsibility, and works to correct the behavior, then he is making progress. If not, then do not harbor false hope. If you want to know how the future will be with him, look at the past. The longer you wait to deal with his problems, the more burdensome they will become. Throughout all of this, he must have some personal motivation to change. All of the impetus should not come from you.

The presence of difficulties does not necessarily mean you need to break things off. It is common for couples to walk away from a relationship if things get tough. Your job is to discern if the issue is significant enough to merit a breakup, or if it is a problem that can be solved. As you pray and ask the Lord for guidance, do not try to figure out the answers on your own. Turn to people you trust, such as family members, a priest, youth minister, or friends. Reflect on their input and have courage.

Whatever your decision, make it clear. The longer it flops back and forth, the worse it is. If you do break things off, do not worry. If he is the right one for you, then taking this time off will not hurt. Also, do not jump back into the relationship quickly if you see signs of improvement in his behavior. A person can manipulate another into letting him back even if he has not made a true change of heart. Resist the temptation, wait on God, and write a letter to yourself about why you broke up, and what you are looking for in a spouse. When you feel the urge to jump back into the relationship for comfort, you will have a reminder of why you are holding out for God's best.

If you break up, you might desire to "just be friends." But as long as one of you is still romantically interested in the other, this is not easy to do. If the two of you are to be friends again one day, you need space right now. When we try the "just friends" approach right after a breakup, it is usually because we are dragging our feet and we do not want to let go. I have tried it before, and it can harm the friendship in the long run because the breakup is so drawn out.

And remember to take this to God in prayer. Ask him what he thinks you should do. Sometimes we run around and grab what we want and rarely sit still long enough to hear him. He will speak if we will listen. Until you do make a decision, live the virtue of purity in the relationship. This will help you to see more clearly. Also, chaste relationships tend to end on a happier note, since the couple did not do anything regrettable.

31

My girlfriend of two years just broke up with me. I thought that she was the one, and I feel crushed. I am not sleeping well, I have lost my appetite, and I can not understand why God would let this happen.

I have been through a couple of tough breakups, and during those times Scripture was a great consolation. God wants us to remember that even when we know nothing about our future, "The Lord is faithful in all his words, and gracious in all his deeds" (Ps. 145:13). The Lord's timing is perfect, and his will is your refuge. His plan will be clear in time, so be still and know that he is God,

74   IF YOU REALLY LOVED ME

that he is faithful, and that he knows exactly what he is doing. "The works of the Lord are all good, and he will supply every need in its hour. And no one can say, 'This is worse than that,' for all things will prove good in their season. So now sing praise with all your heart and voice, and bless the name of the Lord" (Sir. 39:33–35).

It is natural to feel a painful sense of loss during this time, but in the midst of this suffering, do not lose your peace. In the words of St. Paul, "Rejoice always, pray constantly, give thanks in all circumstances; for this is the will of God in Christ Jesus for you" (1 Thess. 5:16–18). The prophet Nehemiah advises, "Do not be grieved, for the joy of the Lord is your strength" (Neh. 8:10). Although rejoicing may be the last thing on your mind right now, God deserves our thanks just as much when times are bad as when everything goes our way. One of the most beautiful forms of praise to God is when we thank him for his providence before we see it unfold. After all, is he less of a good God when we can not fathom his ways?

So take this time to draw closer to God and rest in him. As Psalm 62 says, "My soul rests in God alone" (Psalm 62:1, NAB). The more our peace depends on human beings, the more we will realize that another human being can never satisfy us. I sometimes imagine a little throne on top of the human heart, and we get to decide who sits there. We often place people there, and if things go well with them, life is beautiful. When things go wrong, and they do not reciprocate affection, or say just the right thing, then we lose our peace. Only God deserves to sit on this throne, and only he can hold it in peace.

This is not to say that once we put him there, nothing affects us. Trusting him does not mean that we will never have feelings of hurt or confusion. It simply means that in the midst of the storm, we remain at peace even when it seems like Jesus is asleep (see Mark 4:35–41). Now is a good time to make sure that all is in order in your life and that doing God's will is your number one priority. Sometimes we are so anxious about our relationships with others that we forget that the most important relationship in our lives must be our friendship with God. Pray that you may be single-hearted for the Lord as King David was.

Also, know that your suffering is not in vain. When you accept suffering, you can join it to the sufferings of Christ and offer it as a prayer. The apostle Paul said, "Now I rejoice in my sufferings for your sake, and in my flesh I complete what is lacking in Christ's afflictions for the sake of his body, that is, the church" (Col. 1:24). If you need a suggestion regarding what to offer your sufferings for, I would ask that you offer some of them as a prayer for all of the teens I speak to about chastity. You can save many souls through your suffering, although many people do not realize this. So suffer well, be still, and trust the Lord. "There are years that ask questions, and there are years that answer."

3

Preparing for Marriage

32

How do you know if you should marry the person you are seeing?

The most important decision you will make in life is to follow God. The second most important decision is your vocation. So make sure that God is guiding your choice. Talk to him about your dreams, your joys, your problems, and your fears. It is common to meet people who have faith in God, but they select a spouse on their own, get engaged, and then only afterwards ask God and their family to bless it. Try that the other way—start with God and your family—and it tends to run more smoothly.

Here are five practical points to consider when wondering if you should marry a specific person.

One: How is your friendship? It is easy to feel close to a person if you have been physically intimate, but apart from the physical element, how well can you honestly say you know this person? The more physically involved you have been, the more you will need to step back to evaluate the relationship. This is because physical intimacy clouds our judgment—which it should. One of the benefits of total physical intimacy for married couples is that it renders them less critical of each other. However, this clouding of your thinking belongs in marriage, not before.

Be honest in examining what truly unites the two of you. Is it a desire for pleasure or emotional gain? Is there an unhealthy dependency, where one or both of you have made an idol out of marriage, expecting that it will solve loneliness? How do the two of you deal with differences? Can you disagree lovingly, or are there some issues of manipulation, anger, or guilt that need to be sorted out first? Before marriage it is easy to maintain a good image, so make sure you have seen each other with your masks down, so to speak. Lastly, is there a real romantic interest? Some people say that romantic feelings are not that important, but there is grave reason for concern if these feelings are not present. This is not to say that you must feel constantly madly in love with each other. Most people do not struggle with the absence of feelings, but with infatuation. Just have the honesty to look at where you stand with this.

Two: Are the two of you on the same page when it comes to the size of your family? Does one of you expect one child, while the other envisions three minivans brimming with kids? Does one of you want kids right away while the other wants to wait ten years before having any children? If you have different dreams, then now is the time to be honest about your differences. More importantly, do you think that your prospective spouse would be a good parent?

Three: Are you financially ready for a family? The book of Proverbs advises, "Prepare your work outside, get everything ready for you in the field; and after that build your house" (Prov. 24:27). We should not jump into marriage before we are able to financially care for a family. You do not need to have college money set aside for your kids before you get married, but you should be stable enough with your career that you will be able to carry the great responsibilities that come with the blessings of parenthood. [65]

Four: How is your prospective spouse's faith? Do you lead each other to God? Is your relationship centered on God? Do the two of you have different faiths? Does he or she have a faith at all? The Bible advises against marrying a non-believer (2 Cor. 6:14) because marriage is difficult enough without having differences on an issue that should be the foundation of your life together. If one goes to a non-Catholic church, then know that there will be trials as a result of this. The Church does allow mixed marriages, but advises against them because of the difficulties that they present within marriage.

In the words of a wise and holy priest, Fr. Marcel Maciel,

"The greater the spiritual compatibility between the two of you, the greater your harmony in marriage will be." [66]

As a result of spiritual compatibility, a husband and wife should be able to do more for God together than they can do apart. They should form a team, and to be effective they need to have the same goal in mind. So, take this all to prayer and trust that God will guide you. Some couples make the mistake of failing to ask for the Lord's guidance, while others over-spiritualize the matter and will not move forward unless they receive numerous signs from heaven. God wants you to have confidence. Trust in him, and as Augustine said, "Love God, and do as you will." Use all the wisdom at your disposal, and then make a decision.

Five: What do your friends and families say? It is easy for a couple to become isolated and fail to consult the friends and families God has given them. They know your habits, your emotional health, your dreams, and plenty of things you probably wish nobody knew. But they love you nonetheless and can give some of the best guidance.

As I was finishing my masters studies, I was seeing a young woman and we were looking toward marriage. We met with her parents to discuss our hopes. The parents approved of our relationship, but saw marriage as something still several years ahead of us. At the time, I was frustrated that they could not see how much we loved each other, but their wisdom prevailed and the Lord took us down different paths. Her family had a great deal of wisdom, and they knew that if we were to be together we would have to be patient and prayerful, waiting for the proper time.

Finally, know that if marriage is anything, it is a carefully planned leap of faith. You will need to weigh all of the above considerations and more, pray about them, and move ahead. You can only know a person so well before you marry. This is because coming to know another person is not so much a destination as it is a lifelong process. Within marriage you will see strengths and weaknesses more clearly than ever before. Because of this, there are inevitably going to be disappointments, but you should anticipate them with hope.

When difficulties arise—and they will come—they will test and affirm your love. Marriage is not an endless whirling romance, and your marriage will suffer to the extent that you expect it to fit that fairy tale. When the infatuation fades, some imagine that they must not have married Mr. or Miss Right. This is partly why the majority of divorces happen within the first two years of marriage. It is a shame that couples are not prepared to let their relationship breathe. We often have little faith when the time comes to exhale. There is a love waiting to grow, but it is a quieter love than a couple knows at the start of their relationship. It is unfortunate that so few have the patience to wait and work in sacrifice to see it blossom.

Successful marriages are not the result of finding the perfect person, but of loving the imperfect person that you have chosen to marry. Do not allow yourself to be discouraged when you discover faults and annoyances that you never recognized before. It is said that after marriage, the man gets upset because the woman changes, and the woman gets upset because the man will not change. But when faults do come to the surface, we should not be set on "fixing" our spouse. We marry a person, not a project. We marry a human being, not an idealized image. Only when we let go of the idealized image and begin to accept and love our spouse will the deepest and most fulfilling kind of love appear.

When a couple understands these principles, they are mature enough to think about marriage. We are not eleven years old any more, fluttering from one crush to another according to how fun the feelings are. When a relationship is based on an infatuation instead of a decision, it will last only as long as the infatuation does. We must be careful about what we base our relationships on, because finding the love that everyone longs for is a serious endeavor.

Pope John Paul II beautifully sums up all of these thoughts in his book *Love and Responsibility*:

The essential reason for choosing a person must be personal, not merely sexual. Life will determine the value of a choice and the value and true magnitude of love. It is put to the test most severely when the sensual and emotional reactions themselves grow weaker, and sexual values as such lose their effect. Nothing then remains except the value of the person, and the inner truth about the love of those connected comes to light. If their love is a true gift of self, so that they belong to the other, it will not only survive but grow stronger, and sink deeper roots. Whereas if it was never more than a synchronization of sensual and emotional experiences it will lose its *raison d'être* [reason for existence] and the persons involved in it will suddenly find themselves in a vacuum. We must never forget that only when love between human beings is put to the test can its true value be seen. [67]

33

Divorce runs in my family, so I do not want to get married. Is that okay?

I do not think that you are really opposed to marriage, you are just afraid of getting a divorce. There is a big difference. I would imagine that the desire to give yourself completely to another and to receive the total gift of another is still in your heart. But because of the marriages you have seen, you have an understandable fear that a love like this is out of your reach. Do not be afraid.

While it is fine never to marry and to live the single or religious life instead, look at your intentions for avoiding marriage. Each vocation is a calling, and each requires courage, love, and sacrifice. God may call you to the married life and ask you to trust him despite all the failed marriages you have seen. Just as there has been a rash of broken marriages in your family, perhaps God plans on using you to turn the tide for future generations. There is no reason why you need to follow in your parents' footsteps when you can make the decision to love so that your kids will want to follow in yours.

If we want a great marriage, we need to start building love's foundation now. Unfortunately, most people seem to spend more time preparing for their wedding than they do for their marriage.

If we start disciplining ourselves now, we will have a firm foundation on which to build a lifelong love.

This is what I mean by preparation. While in high school, I spent countless hours in batting cages. On one afternoon I hit thirty-eight consecutive rounds with the eighty mile-per-hour pitching machine—which adds up to 684 swings. When I finished, my back was sore and I had blood blisters on my hands, but I did not mind because it was a time of serious training. You could have told me this was "repressive" training and that I should free myself from it, but it was not. I had a goal in mind. When I made my college baseball team as a freshman, I thought I had reached my goal, but the training had just begun. We would practice six or seven days a week for several hours at a time (not including games). This preparation was essential if we ever hoped to have a successful season.

Unfortunately, some couples spend less time getting ready for a lifetime of marriage than we spent preparing for a few months of baseball. If I wanted a good batting average, I would train myself to read a pitcher and hit his curve. If we want successful marriages, we need to train ourselves in the virtues that hold marriage together: humility, servanthood, purity, honesty, faithfulness, and the like. Begin fostering these virtues in your life now, and you will have more confidence in the hope of a lasting love. Then, if God chooses to call you to a vocation other than marriage, you will have the peace of knowing that you did not avoid marriage because of fear, but embraced another vocation because you heard his voice and followed it.

34

What role does physical attraction play in a decision to date someone? Should a person value personality more than attraction?

Being attracted to another person is wonderful, and I would not recommend that a couple get married if they are not attracted to each other. This is the natural way God that has made us. However, if a woman marries a man only because of an intense physical attraction, or a man refuses to get married because he can not find a Christian Barbie doll, then there is a problem. We are not to expect flawless perfection in the other. If we do, then the flaw is not in the others, but in us. We may need to readjust our priorities so that love does not pass us by. As one man said, "God help the man who will not marry until he finds a perfect woman, and God help him still more if he finds her." [68]

The book of Proverbs says: "Like a golden ring in a swine's snout is a beautiful woman with a rebellious disposition. . . . Charm is deceptive and beauty fleeting; the woman who fears the Lord is to be praised" (Prov. 11:22, 31:30, NAB). These verses do not mean that physical attraction is bad, but that other factors, such as the person's personality and spirituality, are more important. When the beauty fades—and the external beauty will fade —then who are you left with? Ask yourself this question now instead of later. Look at a same-sex grandparent of the person you would like to marry. Now add all the internal qualities that your potential spouse has. Can you say that you would still be attracted to him or her? You should be. An easier way to test your attraction is to pretend that you are blind. Now ask yourself how attractive the other becomes.

A relationship stands on whatever foundation you choose. If a couple builds their relationship on the foundation of pleasure, the relationship will last as long as the pleasure is sufficient. If it is based only upon looks, then when the looks fade, so will the relationship. Since judgment is easily clouded by physical beauty and the infatuation it inspires, make sure you have mentors who can provide you with guidance.

35

I really like the dating scene and the freedom to see different women without having to settle down and get married. Is that okay?

I think that you need to take an honest look at your motives. When you enter into these temporary relationships, what is your goal? The natural response may be to say that you date around simply to have a good time. But ask yourself if perhaps these short relationships are a shield for you. Do they cover up a deeper fear that you might not be able to have a lasting relationship? Is it a way to guard your heart from becoming too involved with the demands of love? We men must have the courage to meet those demands if we intend to hold the heart of a woman. This may be risky and painful for us, but as C. S. Lewis wrote, "The only place outside heaven where you can be perfectly safe from all the dangers and perturbations of love is hell." [69]

I once read that "Young love is a flame; very pretty, very hot and fierce, but still only light and flickering. The love of the older and disciplined heart is as coals, deep-burning and unquenchable." [70] If you want to find unquenchable love, you must come to grips with the fact that love is not free. It costs everything, but this total gift of ourselves is precisely what makes us most free. It liberates us from the prison of doing everything for our own sake. Otherwise we will die having learned to love no one but ourselves. In the words of Pope John Paul II, love "draws one out of the shell of individualism and egocentrism." [71] It sounds weird but we do not know freedom until we give it away for the sake of love. That is why it exists: so that it can be surrendered. If we live for ourselves, we miss the point of our existence, because we have been created to love as God loves.

I would challenge you to not invite the interests of a woman unless you are interested in loving her permanently. Men generally find it easy to grab and conquer when it comes to pleasure and success. But when it comes to giving or committing, we hold back. We fear. We hesitate. But as Pope John Paul II said, "The person who does not decide to love forever will find it very difficult to really love for even one day."[72]

36

I have met this great girl and she is exactly what I have been hoping for. I really want to marry her some day. Do you have any tips for how to keep from messing this up?

Entrust this relationship to God. He is the Master Builder, not you. David wrote, "Unless the Lord builds the house, those who build it labor in vain. Unless the Lord watches over the city, the watchman stays awake in vain. It is in vain that you rise up early and go late to rest, eating the bread of anxious toil; for he gives to his beloved sleep" (Ps. 127:1–2). Also, let the peace of Christ reign in your heart. Your task is to take this to prayer so that you can determine the will of God and follow it.

Where do you start? Build the foundation of a graced friendship before jumping into romance. If and when a relationship starts, you will want to have a clear sense of direction in it, looking toward marriage. After all, this is the reason to date. As for now, there is a lot of wisdom in taking it easy. If it is love, then this time of anticipation will not hurt.

In a relationship that is new and exciting, people often stay up to the wee hours of the morning pouring out their life history and emotional secrets. They feel incredibly close because they know so much about each other's past. Other couples dive headlong into a deep spiritual relationship as well. People in both situations, if they value chastity, also will be working to hold back on the physical side of things. But the intimacy of hearts has moved so fast that the physical side yearns to catch up. Picture a slingshot primed to launch. A similar tension results when you move too fast on emotional matters and then cannot, morally, match that emotional depth with a corresponding physical intimacy. So take it easy. I do not intend to put a damper on love, but to help you pace yourself so that love reaches its fullest potential. Take your time and allow trust to develop and strengthen.

Also, take the initiative to make the relationship godly. At the same time, do not attempt to be her spiritual guru or father in the faith. She is not to be under your tutelage as if she is your student, disciple, or child. It is easy for a good-hearted young man to want to assume these roles for a young woman, especially if she has not been involved in her faith for long. Progress toward God side by side.

Involve your families, and tap into their years of wisdom. One man with a great deal of insight on the topic of relationships is Dr. James Dobson, who offers this advice in his book *Love Must be Tough*:

> Don't let the relationship move too fast in its intimacy. The phrase "too hot not to cool down" has validity. Take it one step at a time. . . . Don't call too often on the phone or give the other person an opportunity to get tired of you. . . . Don't be too quick to reveal your desire to get married—or that you think you have found Mr. Wonderful or Miss Marvelous. If your partner has not arrived at the same conclusion, you will throw him or her into panic. . . . Do not expect anyone to meet *all* of your emotional needs. Maintain interests and activities outside that romantic relationship, even after marriage. . . . In addition to the many moral, spiritual, and physical reasons for remaining virgins until marriage, there are numerous psychological and interpersonal advantages to the exercise of self-control and discipline. Though it's an old-fashioned notion, perhaps, it is still true that men do not respect "easy" women and often become bored with those who have held nothing in reserve. Likewise, women often disrespect men who have only one thing on their minds. Both sexes need to remember how to use a very ancient word. It's pronounced "NO!" [73]

Dobson also notes that the relationship must be able to breathe. Do not be afraid to give each other some space, because relationships thrive best when there is freedom, respect, and confidence. The less one exhibits these characteristics, the more likely he is to have difficulty in romantic endeavors. Lastly, realize that too many people see marriage as a finish line. They often arrive there exhausted, only to discover that the real work has only begun. Making a lifelong love is a demanding task that yields its priceless fruits only to those who have loved with patience and fortitude.

In the meantime, work to better yourself. Becoming a saint is the best gift you could ever give to your wife and children. Work vigorously against your defects and do your best to improve as a man of God each day.

37

Should I move in with my boyfriend before we get married? It seems like a smart move, because you want to really know a person before you commit to life together.

Most cohabiting couples who hope to marry see their arrangement as a good test run, a way to make sure that they are compatible before tying the knot. After all, who wants to go through a divorce?

Aside from all the spiritual factors regarding premarital sex, we should take a look at what researchers have found about living together before marriage. Two researchers summarized the findings of numerous studies by stating that "expectation of a positive relationship between cohabitation and marital stability . . . has been shattered in recent years by studies conducted in several Western countries."[74]

What the studies discovered is this: if you do not want to get divorced, do not move in until after the wedding. Why is that? Consider the following facts about cohabitation: Most couples who live together never end up getting married, but those who do tie the knot are almost twice as likely to divorce as couples who do not live together before marriage.[75] Overall, couples who cohabit before marriage have a divorce rate of about eighty percent,[76] and non-virgin brides are sixty percent more likely to end up divorced than women who enter marriage as virgins.[77] Couples who cohabited prior to marriage have greater marital conflict and poorer communication, and they made more frequent visits to marriage counselors.[78]

Women who cohabited before marriage are more than three times as likely to cheat on their husbands within marriage.[79] The U.S. Justice Department found that women who cohabit are sixty-two times more likely to be assaulted by a live-in boyfriend than by a husband.[80] They were also more than three times as likely to be depressed as married women,[81] and the couples were less sexually satisfied than those who waited for marriage.[82]

From a standpoint of marital duration, marital peace, marital fidelity, physical safety, emotional well-being, and sexual satisfaction, cohabitation is not exactly a recipe for happiness. Even *USA Today* reported, "Could this be true love? Test it with courtship, not cohabitation."[83] You may assume that if the couple had lived together a bit longer, they would have ironed out the difficulties and not had these problems in marriage. The studies show the opposite: longer cohabitations are associated with a higher likelihood of divorce.[84] Even if you do not think that your boyfriend would be abusive or that you would get depressed, the divorce rate speaks for itself.

Like all of us, you dream of a lasting love. If you are serious about making this relationship work, save your marriage before it starts and do not move in until after the wedding.

38

Why are the divorce rates so high for couples who lived together before marriage?

Cohabiting relationships undermine commitment, since it is assumed that if one person finds enough faults in the other, he is free to leave. However, successful marriages are not the result of a lack of annoying qualities in the other; they are the result of choosing to love and forgive the other daily, with all of his or her imperfections. It is the ability to sacrifice that holds marriages together, not the absence of nuisances. Couples who refuse to cohabit before marriage and refuse to engage in premarital sex seem to have a better understanding of the notion of sacrifice than couples who give in.

The desire to "test drive" a marriage demonstrates a lack of understanding regarding what makes a marriage work. It also shows a real lack of faith in one's love for the other. In one sense, the couple is saying that they desire intimacy, but on the other hand they want to leave a way out if the partner does not measure up. This sows seeds of doubt and distrust from the start. Some couples seem to be under the impression that a good relationship will not have disappointments. When they marry and the disappointments come, they often bail out.

As G. K. Chesterton said,

If Americans can be divorced for "incompatibility of temper," I cannot conceive why they are not all divorced. I have known many happy marriages, but never a compatible one. The whole aim of marriage is to fight through and survive the instant when incompatibility becomes unquestionable. For a man and a woman, as such, are incompatible. [85]

If you want a marriage to last, take an honest look at what makes love work. According to Pope John Paul II,

We love the person complete with all his or her virtues and faults, and up to a point, independently of those virtues and in spite of those faults. The strength of such a love emerges most clearly when the beloved person stumbles, when his or her weaknesses or even sins come into the open. One who truly loves does not then withdraw his love, but loves all the more, loves in full consciousness of the other's shortcomings and faults, and without in the least approving of them. [86]

This is why the slogan "love is blind" is off the mark. Infatuation is blind, but love has both eyes wide open. That way we can see and know the other person fully, so that we can love him or her completely. Married couples often say that they really did not know their spouse fully until years into marriage, but dating couples who are infatuated feel that they know everything about each other. It takes a lifetime to truly know the other, and cohabitation is afraid of that task.

If things are running smoothly for a cohabiting couple, they may head toward marriage, thinking, "Well, we haven't been fighting much lately, and after living together for this long, I sure don't want to start over with someone else. Why don't we just make it official?" These couples often find it difficult to explain exactly what marriage is. You go through a big ceremony, get a piece of paper and new Tupperware, and go back to what you were doing before. This undermines the meaning of marriage as a covenant that two people make with God. Since they think less of marriage, they are less likely to work tirelessly to preserve it. Even when cohabiting couples do not end up marrying, their breakup can be as wrenching as an actual divorce.

Some people assume that living together is not a problem as long as the couple is not sleeping together. But there is a problem: they are putting themselves in an occasion of sin. They are also causing scandal (giving bad example) to neighbors, who will reasonably assume they are sleeping together. By living together, they are also saying that they lack confidence in their relationship. Waking up in the same house on a daily basis with a person you love is a gift that should be reserved for marriage. Stealing all the privileges of marriage in advance reminds me of my childhood, when I would beg my parents for early Christmas gifts every day the week prior to Christmas. If they had allowed me to open all but one (which they did not), Christmas would not have seemed that big a deal. The same goes for marriage.

Lastly, consider the fact that Joseph and Mary did not need to cohabit to have an exemplary marriage. So why do we?

39

Is it okay to have sex while you are engaged? After all, you are going to get married anyway.

Engagement is a special time, and during this time couples may feel that they are "almost married," but in reality being married is like being pregnant—you either are or you are not. No matter how committed a couple may feel, until they actually pledge themselves to one another on their wedding day, they cannot pledge themselves to one another with their bodies in bed.

Some might feel that this idea is old-fashioned. It is definitely old, but it still works. As modern research shows, *couples who sleep together before marriage are three times as likely to divorce* as those who waited for marriage.[87] Research also shows much higher rates of adultery among couples who had premarital sex as compared with those who waited.[88]

Waiting to receive each other from the Lord allows the couple to establish authentic intimacy. By waiting on God and focusing on what he is calling them to, the couple receives the freedom to see that intimacy is not simply about how close your body is to someone else's. A healthy relationship does not require sex in order to be intimate. Love is patient. A man and woman who are confident in their love know that they will have the rest of their lives to enjoy sex, but now is their *only* time for preparing for marriage—for laying the foundation for the rest of their lives together.

Waiting to share the gift of sex should not be seen as a passive delay of passion, but an active training in faithfulness. In the words of the *Catechism of the Catholic Church*, "Those who are engaged to marry are called to live chastity in continence [abstinence]. They should see in this time of testing a discovery of mutual respect, an apprenticeship in fidelity, and the hope of receiving one another from God. They should reserve for marriage the expressions of affection that belong to married love. They will help each other grow in chastity."[89]

Don't you want to know *before* the wedding if your spouse will be able to resist temptations *after* the wedding?

Since engagement is a time to prepare to become a sacrament, the months preceding a marriage are a time of serious discernment. By having sex during this time, couples hinder their ability to look clearly at the relationship. They feel so close as a result of sex that they are often unable to critically look at the past, present, or future. The sexual intimacy may even blind them from seeing that their relationship lacks real intimacy, and it may prevent them from bringing to the surface worries or hesitations that they may have. In fact, sex may be covering up defects of love.

Some people ask, "Well, how do you know if you want to marry a person if you don't sleep with her?" I would reply, "How do you know you should marry her once you have slept together?" If anything you are less clear-minded, because *sex is not designed to be a test to find a good spouse.*

Just because a person is capable of physical intimacy, it does not mean that he or she is capable of the other kinds of intimacy that hold a marriage together. Because sex has the power to bond, the experience may seem wonderful in the initial stages of a relationship and both partners will feel quite "compatible." But think about a couple you know who has been married for fifty years. They are sitting there on the front porch swing, smiling with all their wrinkles at each other. Do you think it is because they are so sexually compatible? They are still together because they have been refined by the fires of love, not burnt by the counterfeits of lust.

So why *not* wait for the honeymoon? I know of couples who were sexually active long before their wedding and when they arrived at their honeymoon suite, they immediately fell asleep. They had been there and done that, so why not rest up for something new and exciting—like jet skiing? They only robbed themselves. On the other hand, one woman who saved that gift for the honeymoon said that it was "*unspeakably worth the wait.*" [90] How often do you hear of promiscuous couples experiencing such joy?

If a man and woman refuse to wait, what are their motives?

Does impatience, lust, or pride motivate the couple to disobey God? These vices only harm a marriage. It is through humility, obedience, chastity, patience, and a willingness to sacrifice that a couple builds a lifelong love. So why not practice these virtues now?

In the meantime, know that each time you resist sin you bless one another. In addition, God has issued a special challenge to men. When a man perseveres in the virtue of chastity, he helps fulfill that challenge: to love his bride as Christ loves the Church, to give himself up for her, that he might sanctify her, that he might present his bride to God without spot or wrinkle or any such thing, that she might be holy and without blemish (Eph. 5:25-27). A man should consider his acceptance of this challenge to be the measure of his love for his bride.

If we do not understand these principles, perhaps we do not understand what marriage is. Is it merely a public declaration of the love that a bride and groom feel? Or is God present there, establishing a supernatural bond—a covenant with them that can only be severed by death? Does the Holy Spirit actually do something to that man and woman as they exchange their vows or is the wedding a decorative formality?

At every sacramental marriage, an invisible spiritual reality *will* take place on that altar, changing a man to a husband and a woman to a wife. The couple enters into a union that is a sacrament. That night, the marital embrace will become the visible expression of this invisible union ratified by God. Until the marriage vows have been said, a woman is not a wife and should not be treated as one. This is especially important to remember, since half of all engagements break off.

When a husband gives his body to his bride and a bride gives herself to him, their bodies speak the truth: "I am entirely yours." On the other hand, sex anywhere but in marriage is dishonest. No matter what, it cannot say, "I am entirely yours." Therefore, having sex during the engagement is not a matter of "peeking under the wrapping paper." It is a matter of completely missing the point of sex and marriage.

If you are engaged, ponder for a moment the gift of your partner. Look how generous God has been with you. When you come to the altar, do you not want to give God a gift in return? Make the sacrifice to keep your engagement pure, so that you come to the altar with this gift for him.

40

If an unmarried couple gets pregnant, should they get married?

There is no simple answer to this, since each situation and relationship is different. What I would recommend in most cases is that the couple wait at least until the child is born to make a decision. There is so much to consider in those nine months that the couple will not be in the best frame of mind to discern marriage.

There are at least four options that are open to the couple: to place the child for adoption and have the couple go their separate ways; to place the baby for adoption but stay open to marriage; to get married and raise the child together; or to keep the baby and not get married. All four options will be difficult, so it is important that the couple seek the best advice they can find. By talking to parents, priests, and counselors at crisis pregnancy centers (see resource section), the couple will be able to make the best decision for the child and for themselves.

41

I am in college and met a great woman, but she is already been married and divorced. Is it wrong to date her?

There are a couple of things to consider here. If she was married and her spouse is still alive and their marriage has not been annulled, then for practical purposes she is not available for you to date. You must consider her a married woman, regardless of whether the state recognizes them as legally married or whether she no longer lives with her husband. When a person is married,

they are married until death. Only if the Church determines that
her presumed marriage was never actually a valid marriage at all
can she be considered available while her former partner still lives.

This is why Jesus said, "Whoever divorces his wife and marries another, commits adultery against her" (Mark 10:11). This
includes doing anything with a divorced person that you would
not do with a married person. This is a difficult saying, but it
came from the mouth of the Lord.

42

Isn't an annulment the same as a divorce?

No. A divorce is a legal decree that a valid, legal marriage has been
done away with. In the eyes of the state, a marriage can be real and
still be dissolved. The Church, however, recognizes that before
God a valid marriage between two baptized people can *never* be
dissolved; that spouses are bound to one another as long as they
live. An annulment, therefore, is not a decree that this bond has
been dissolved, but that, on investigation, no marriage bond ever
existed.

When two people seek to be united in Christian marriage, certain realities must be present in order for that union to take effect.
For example, if one partner is being forced into the marriage, or
if one does not intend to be faithful, or to be open to children, he
or she is not entering what God considers a marriage. Therefore,
the marriage is not valid no matter what the state may think about
it. (There are other conditions, but I mention these for starters.)

Imagine that a couple went through a wedding ceremony, but
the bride was being forced to marry the groom. Even though it
looked like a wedding, there was no valid marriage. Since there
was never a marriage to begin with, they are not bound to each
other. Their "marriage" could be declared null—found by the
Church to have no existence in the eyes of God. Since God has
not joined them together, they are still free to be validly married to other parties. Even Jesus spoke of this in the Gospel of

Matthew, when he forbade divorce and remarriage, "unless the [first] marriage is unlawful," i.e., null (Matt. 19:9, NAB).

So an annulment does not end a real marriage, but declares that there never was a sacramental marriage to begin with. The Church goes through a long investigation to determine if the marriage was validly contracted. If it was, then even if the marriage turned sour years later, the Church cannot dissolve that. (The couple may separate if necessary, such as in the case of abuse, and even may obtain a civil divorce, but neither is free to remarry.) When a valid marriage has taken place between two baptized persons, only death can sever that bond.

43

Did Jesus say that everyone's marriage would be ended in heaven? I thought that what God has joined no one could separate.

In Matthew 22:30 Jesus said that in heaven, people are neither married, nor are they given in marriage. In order to see God's ultimate plan for the sacrament of marriage, we need to understand what marriage is.

A sacrament is a sign that Jesus established in order to give us grace. By spousal love, the married couple makes visible to the world the love that God has for all of us. God's plan for humanity is that mankind be united to him in a way that is similar to the way husbands and wives are united to each other. That is why the Church is called the Bride of Christ, and the Bible describes heaven as a wedding banquet. In marriage, couples are living images of this deeper spiritual reality. This is God's vision and purpose for every marriage!

But as great as weddings are, they are just shadows of the reality of the one eternal marriage. Earthly marriages were created for earth, but as St. Paul says, "When the perfect comes, the imperfect will pass away" (1 Cor. 13:10). When a married couple goes to heaven, the sacramental marriage (like all other sacraments) will pass away and be fulfilled by the reality that it now points to or veils. So we *will* have marriage in heaven: The union of us all as the bride of Christ with the heavenly Bridegroom at the eternal wedding banquet. This life is the engagement, and heaven is the consummation.

Marriage is intended both for the raising of children and to promote the good of the spouses, including their growth in holiness. Since everyone is perfected in holiness in heaven and everyone will have already been born, the purposes of marriage will have been completed. So where does this leave married couples when they get to heaven? Because sin will be gone and everyone will be filled with God's love, those who were husband and wife in this life will be able to love one another with an intensity never known to them while on earth. They will live like the angels, in continual worship of God. They are the bride of Christ, and even if their earthly marriage was not made in heaven, it will be fulfilled there.

4

How Far is Too Far?

44

Is it wrong to flirt with guys?

Flirting means different things for different age groups. When I was in second grade, if I liked a girl, I would throw a rock at her. (Fortunately for women, I have since made some progress in this area.) When we matured to the fourth grade, things got more sophisticated: A girl would ask her friend to pass a note to a boy, inviting him to check the appropriate box if he was interested in her. By sixth grade, the tactics were more refined, and a girl might have her friend "accidentally" shove her into a cute boy as they walked out of class. This is all amusing, but by junior high, the girls leave the notes behind as they start to realize what interests guys. This is when flirting can become a problem.

The basic definition of "flirt" is to tease or toy with another; to pay amorous attention to someone without serious intentions. To the degree that one is being impure or dishonest, flirting is wrong. There is nothing intrinsically wrong with letting another person know that you are attracted to him. The problem comes when you lead him on for the sake of amusement or to boost your self-esteem, usually while causing him to have impure thoughts or desires.

If you are attracted to another, be pure and honest in your dealings with him and the Lord will bless your friendship. There is nothing wrong with being playful with the person and going out of your way to meet him. Just make sure your tactics are done with integrity. If you are an affectionate girl, be careful about how you express this. A guy might perceive your affection as a hint that you want him to do more with you. This is because affection usually does not come naturally for guys. It is out of the ordinary, and so the guy may associate it with something sexual.

The best approach is to make your intentions for purity clear, and make sure that your words, your actions, and your outfits convey the same message. Also consider this: Lots of guys will date a flirt, but who wants to marry one? If a girl is flirty toward me, what reason do I have to think that she is not flirting with other guys? A girl is much more attractive if she does not flutter around trying to impress everyone.

One reason a girl may be a flirt is because she wants to be loved. The attention might soothe a wounded self-esteem, but in the end it is like trying to survive on a diet of cotton candy: it tastes sweet but leaves her malnourished. Only God can heal those deep wounds. When a young woman sits still long enough to hear God and when she sees with her heart how he looks at her with love, she recognizes the lewd comments and looks from various guys as nothing more than counterfeit love.

As Mother Teresa said, "Stay close to Jesus. He loves you." By the side of Christ a woman finds her independence. When she stands beside Christ, and he reveals her worth to her, she no longer depends on the approval of random guys to build her self-worth.

44

Is French kissing a mortal sin? Everyone I talk to gives me a different answer.

First we should define a mortal sin. A mortal sin is an act that cuts the life of God out of your soul. Scripture speaks of this in 1 John 5:17: "All wrongdoing is sin, but there is sin which is not mortal." For a sin to be mortal, three conditions must be met: 1. The sin must involve grave matter; 2. The person must have sufficient reflection and knowledge of its sinfulness; 3. The person freely consents to it anyway. If any of these three categories is missing, then the sin is not mortal. Certain things such as ignorance, addiction, and immaturity can lessen the culpability (guiltiness) of a particular offense, but we can not use these things as a license to indulge in sin.

Now, to the issue of French kissing. I do not think it would be right to say that every person who has ever French kissed outside of marriage committed a mortal sin. But some people have sinned mortally by French kissing. But before we try to determine how serious a sin French kissing could be, we should look at why it could be sinful at all. Many people think, "If it's a mortal sin, then I don't want to do it. But if it's a venial sin . . . then I don't want to miss it!"

We need to drop this minimalist idea that focuses on how much we can get away with before we offend God. Even the smallest sin divides, while purity ignites true love. Elisabeth Elliott wrote in her book *Passion and Purity*, "How shall I speak of a few careless kisses to a generation nurtured on the assumption that nearly everybody goes to bed with everybody. Of those who flounder in the sea of permissiveness and self-indulgence, are there any who still search the sky for the beacon of purity? If I did not believe there were, I would not bother to write." [91]

I used to take for granted that everyone knew that French kissing is sexually arousing, especially for a guy. But I have met women who act surprised when they find out that a man is sexually aroused by passionate kissing (or before then). French kissing is deeply unitive, since the penetration of one person into another is part of becoming one with him or her physically. This passionate kissing tells a man's body that it should prepare for intercourse, and when a man is aroused, generally he is not satisfied until he is relieved. Therefore, French kissing teases the body with desires that can not be morally satisfied outside of marriage. For the couple that is saving sex for marriage, French kissing is like a fifteen-year-old sitting in a car in his driveway, revving up the engine, and slamming on the brakes because he knows he does not have the license to drive.

Nevertheless, some say that French kissing is really no big deal and it does not mean anything. But the more of ourselves we give away, the less we value the gift of our body and our entire self (and people will respond by treating us with less respect as well). Ask yourself what your kisses are worth. Are they a way to repay a guy for a nice evening? Are they a solution to boredom on a date? Are they a way to cover up hurts or loneliness? Even worse, are they merely for "harmless" fun? If the answer to any of these questions is yes, then we have forgotten the purpose of a kiss and the meaning of intimacy. So do not segregate parts of your sexuality as "no big deal." Your entire body is an infinitely big deal, and this includes your kisses. If we realize this, the simplest of kisses becomes priceless and brings more joy than one hundred one-night stands.

The first relationships I was in during high school, I did not think twice about this kind of kissing. I thought that pleasure was pretty much the same thing as love, so passionate kissing must be really loving. When my relationships matured and deepened and I began taking them to prayer, I gave up this kind of kissing. When I gave it up, it was not because I was convinced at the time that it was really sinful, but because I noticed that it was the first step on a path I did not want to take. It was also pushing other aspects of the relationship to the side. I knew in my heart I could not say with confidence that this kind of intimacy was pleasing to God.

So I had a talk with a girlfriend at the outset of a relationship and we agreed to sacrifice that. This was a huge blessing and I was immediately able to see that the relationship was more holy and joyful. We were not perfect, but I saw for the first time that the more passionate kissing there was in my relationships, the less there was of everything else. This was not something I could understand until I gave it up.

I encourage you to give it a shot. Give up French kissing until you are married. If you have a difficult time accepting this, then have the honesty to ask yourself why. Let's be blunt: If you were forbidden to put your tongue in your boyfriend's mouth, would that hinder your ability to love him? Would not being able to French kiss your girlfriend hinder your ability to glorify God or to lead her to heaven? How much of our intentions are directed toward our gratification, and how much to God's glorification? This is what sexual morality is about: glorifying God with your body. The way you use your sexuality should reflect your love for God and should express the love of God to others. If an area seems gray, then do not go there. Do everything and only those things that you confidently know glorify God. Sure, this is difficult, but love is willing to sacrifice big things as well as small ones for the good of the beloved.

As to what kind of kissing is good, or how much is too much, this is something that each person should take to prayer. More and more often I hear of couples who saved their first kiss for the wedding day. At first this sounded extreme to me, but then I noticed that they were not giving up kissing on the lips because it was bad or because they could not control themselves, but because they cherished a simple kiss so much that they wanted God and the world to witness their first one. Their first kiss could be offered as a prayer.

46

Is oral sex okay, so that you do not go all the way?

If you are being called to marriage, then right now your future spouse is somewhere out there. Do you ever wonder what she or he is doing right now? Maybe he is running the bases during baseball practice, or maybe she is laughing with friends at a coffee shop as they cram for a test. Suppose that he or she is elsewhere, namely at the house of a person who finds him or her very attractive. The parents are not home, and as you read this, that person is trying to talk your future spouse into having oral sex.

If you could speak to the heart of your future spouse right now, would you say, "Oh, go ahead—just make sure you don't go all the way, honey!" Probably not. You would also have some words for the other person, such as: "That's my bride!" or "That's the man who will one day kiss my children goodnight." You would feel sickened by what that person is trying to get from your future husband or wife.

But what about oral sex within marriage? Provided the spouses use it as foreplay leading to intercourse, it is allowed. But it is never to be used as an alternative to intercourse. Sex between a husband and wife is supposed to involve a total gift of self that is open to life. Oral sex can not do either.

One reason why oral sex is gaining popularity is because people think that it is a safe alternative to sex. Although you will not get pregnant from it, it is anything but safe. I once asked a microbiologist which STDs you could *not* get by means of oral sex. She stood there thinking for a while and said, "I can't think of *any* that you can't get from oral sex (including HIV)." Considering that cases of oral herpes and oral gonorrhea are skyrocketing, oral sex is anything but safe. [92]

Other people resort to oral sex so that they do not lose their virginity. Although you do not *technically* lose your virginity by having oral sex, it still robs you of innocence and puts you in situations where you could easily lose your virginity. It does not relieve sexual tension in a man, but creates it and reinforces in him the myth that he has sexual "needs" that must be met, even at the expense of a woman's dignity and innocence.

We need to take an honest look at our motives. Why are we doing this anyway? Why would a person become upset if he or she were not allowed to have oral sex? Recently I was invited to speak to a high school morality class. When I arrived, the teacher said to me in front of the class, "We've been having a big debate about oral sex. They do not see anything wrong with it. What would you say?" Everyone in the class looked at me and awaited my response. I said what came to mind: "If a guy needs to place his genitals into the mouth of his girlfriend in order to show her what she means to him, then it shows exactly what she means to him."

47

Is foreplay with your boyfriend wrong, even if you really love him and just want to get as close as physically possible? I see myself marrying him some day.

Although I was not alive in the 1960s, I understand that at the time there was a big "free love" movement. Apparently, it had one fatal flaw: The promoters of this sexual revolution had no idea what constituted freedom or love. The people assumed that if there were mutual feelings between two people, they should be free to have sex. I agree that we should be free to do whatever love calls us to do, but we need to make sure that it is love that is calling us. It is easy to be moved by infatuation, loneliness, or lust and to mistake any of these for love because the feelings are so strong. Many people assume that if a couple has a strong desire to be sexually intimate, then that is a sign of love indicating they should do whatever they both feel comfortable with.

If you deeply love a person, are committed to him, and see yourself marrying him, why can't you express that in whatever way you want? After all, when you love someone, you desire union with him. I would say that as long as a couple only *sees* themselves being together for life, and can only *talk* about marriage, then they should only *see* themselves having marital relations in the future, within marriage. Until the reality of marriage is there, the expression of marital oneness is dishonest. Even if I reserve sexual arousal for a person whom I hope to marry, this does not make my actions moral.

You mentioned that you wanted to get as close as physically possible. Many young women suspect that this will draw a guy closer to them but this tactic often backfires. As one girl said, "I tried to achieve 'maximum pleasure,' but was becoming painfully disappointed when I found only guilt instead of freedom, pain instead of love, and suffering instead of pleasure. Instead of drawing my boyfriend and me closer together, a sexual relationship only drove us further and further apart."[93]

Perhaps the easiest way to find out if our actions conform to authentic love is to imagine God sitting on a nearby sofa watching us. If his presence would cause immediate shame or the desire to stop dead in our tracks, we need to ask ourselves why. If God is love, and we "really love" the other person, shouldn't we be thrilled to have Love himself witness everything that we do together?

That awkwardness in our hearts is there because deep inside we know that our actions are not fully loving. There are two essential elements of love. The first is the desire for union. (I would say you have got that.) The second and more important element of love is to desire what is best for the other, to desire God and heaven for him. It elevates the desire for union so that the two want to be together not only for a night, but for eternity. Both elements must be present for love to exist. If I crave unity with a girlfriend, but I do not desire her salvation, call it whatever you want, it is not love.

If you are unsure whether or not a particular action could be sinful, then love demands that you refuse to go there. Suppose I put a teaspoon of powder into a cup of tea for a girlfriend. I look at the bowl where I got the powder. It reads "sugar" on one side and "rat poison" on the other. Do I say, "Oh, it's probably not poison. I'll give it to her anyway?" If I loved her, then I would never do something that was possibly lethal for her. Similarly, even if I were not convinced that a particular action with her would be sinful, I would still avoid it if there is good reason to believe that it might be harmful to her soul. Since her soul is more important than her body, I should have all the more concern to protect her salvation.

Also, consider the heart of this guy's future wife, in case you do not end up marrying him. I think that most sincere people who become physically intimate before marriage can see themselves marrying their partner. But most do not end up marrying each other. I have been in a few long relationships, and in each one marriage was a real possibility. In one case, we were even trying on rings. The Lord had different plans for us. Not long ago, I went to her wedding where she married a friend of mine! Watching them exchange vows and kiss at the altar made me take a deep look at the relationships that I have had in my life. Take the same look, and honestly ask yourself if your actions are in any way defrauding the future bride of the guy you are with.

48

Is it okay to hook up with a girl even if we are not dating?

The term "hooking up" can mean a lot of things, but it always means some kind of casual sexual contact, up to and including intercourse itself. Regardless of what you mean by it, you should not be having sexual contact of any sort with a person you are not married to. Even if you both like it, it shows mutual disrespect because you are exchanging a sign of commitment, love, and unity that does not exist.

Speaking of such relationships, Pope John Paul II said, "Deep within yourself, listen to your conscience which calls you to be pure . . . a home is not warmed by the fire of pleasure which burns quickly like a pile of withered grass. Passing encounters are only a caricature of love; they injure hearts and mock God's plan." [94] In the long run, no one benefits from these kinds of relationships. I read of one young husband who said, "I would do anything, ANYTHING, to forget the sexual experiences I had before I met my wife. . . . The pictures of the past and the other women go through my head, and it's killing any intimacy. The truth is, I have been married to this wonderful woman for eight years and I have never been 'alone' in the bedroom with her." [95]

When you "hook up" for fun, physical intimacy begins to lose its depth, greatness, sacredness, and power to bond two people. Sex is shared as easily as a handshake, and the couple loses all reverence for the sacredness of each other's body. You begin thinking that physical pleasure is basically for fun, and can solve the problem of boredom or loneliness. This leads to the idea that if two people agree to do X, then it is okay to do it. Often, this is nothing more than two people agreeing to use each other for mutual gratification. They receive the physical pleasure of being held, the emotional pleasure of being desired, and they remain together so long as they are a source of pleasure for each other. This is not far from prostitution.

You both desire and deserve love. But as long as you are treating one another as objects, you will never be satisfied because neither of you is giving or receiving real love. Have the courage to admit your mistakes with a woman, and do not fall back into the habit of using them, or letting yourself be used. If you can not lead a woman to holiness when you are not that interested in her, how will you lead a woman to God when you are head over heels in love with her? If you can be trusted with the smaller things, you will be responsible with the larger ones. When you do meet someone you are seriously interested in, take it slow. Intense physical intimacy at the beginning of a relationship is a cover-up for the absence of love that failed to develop. The real love that you long for takes patience and purity. Never forget that purity is the guardian of love.

49

How come everyone blames the guys? Girls today are just as sexually aggressive.

Men often receive the blame because we bear a particular responsibility for the wounds inflicted on women. Like it or not, there is no way around this. The world has a double standard. A guy is considered a "player" when he is sexually active, but a woman who lives the same lifestyle is called a "slut."

Nevertheless, the pressure goes both ways. There is no doubt that there are many young women who are more sexually aggressive than their dates. But take a look at the reasons why. When a guy is sexually aggressive, it is usually because he is giving in to his body's strong desires. With young women, there seems to be a different motive. Look into the heart of a young girl who is forward and physical. Odds are, she has been used before, and now she shuts off her emotions from her physical actions. Many men have no qualms about having a one-night stand because they are more able to perform the sexual act as if it were merely a physical event.

Women's hearts and bodies tend to be more integrated. One girl said, "Most of all, at the gut level, there was a desire for intimacy, a desire for marriage, a desire for commitment, a desire for fulfillment and a desire to hear the words 'I accept you.' . . . As an attempt to find fulfillment and acceptance, 'rolling in and out of bed' became a common pattern for me, a balm to cover my fears. Fulfillment took the scope of a few hours instead of what I had imagined—a lifetime. The fears produced the truth: I had become bored *and* boring; I didn't find any lasting acceptance of me; I didn't find my ideal mate from bedroom gymnastics."[96]

When you find a woman who is having one-night stands, you will notice that it is often a kind of protection for her heart. She has been hurt before. She may have no boundaries when it comes to her body but there is a mile-high wall around her heart. She stoops to the level of a temporary physical relationship to prove that she can be as carefree about sex as some men are. It keeps her from having to be vulnerable, and it gives her a false sense of being in control of her life. She is losing the ability to bond, but it is all an effort to numb the interior wounds and find something that feels like love in order to smother the emptiness.

This is known in some circles as "liberation." One man noted, "Most young women strike me as sad, lonely, and confused; hoping for something more, they are not enjoying their hard-won sexual liberation as much as liberation theory says they should."[97] When a young woman encounters the inevitable hurt that accompanies the misuse of sex, she may shut men out of her life or immerse herself in physical relationships in order to forget the wounds of her heart. Imagine that a woman spilled ink on a white carpet. The stain runs deep, so instead of taking the time and effort to scrub it out, she dyes the whole carpet the same color as the ink. This makes the original stain much less noticeable.

That is what is going on in so many hearts. A woman who has been broken from sexual encounters tends to minimize the hurt. One way to do this is to jump into numerous affairs as if it were no big deal. By doing this, she hopes to convince herself that there is no need for healing. One high school girl told me why she had done all sorts of things with guys: "I was only doing it because I had this total and complete lack of love in my life."

Some young women may lower their standards in order to meet a guy, so that they will feel desirable and worth something. In the words of *Complete Woman* magazine, one of the positive aspects of first date sex is that it "makes you briefly forget your huge self-esteem problems."[98] Women know that guys like sex. So sex becomes bait to win the attention of a man. Other young women may once have been reserved about sexual matters, but because of a mistake or a wound from the past, they figure they no longer deserve a good guy. A girl like this may even assume that a man does not like her unless he makes sexual advances toward her. As you see in all these cases, the physical tends to be an avenue for the fulfillment, burial, or protection of the emotional.

50

Exactly how far is too far to go with a girl? Be specific.

I will give some specifics, but before I do, we should lay down a foundation. If we are asking how close to sin we can get girls, we are asking the wrong question. We need a change of heart. We need to start asking, "How close to God can I get her? How far can I go to lead this girl to holiness and guard her innocence?" Until we have this transformation of our heart and will, it will be difficult to determine where to set the physical boundaries in a relationship. Also, whenever we operate with the "how far is too far" mentality, where do we usually end up? More often than not, we end up going right up to that boundary, and inching it forward each time we visit it.

We need to remind ourselves that purity is not simply a matter of staying on one side of a line that we have drawn. It is a battle for our hearts and minds as well as our bodies. Just because a guy has not crossed a line, it does not mean that he is pure. It may mean that he has never had the opportunity to cross it.

Anyway, here are a few guidelines for how you can know how far is too far. Whenever you are considering doing something with a girl, ask yourself if you would do that if Jesus were in the room. In our hearts, we all know what is pleasing to God. Also, consider how you would want a guy to treat your future daughter or future bride and treat women accordingly. Let this sink in. Often, we get so involved in intense relationships that it is hard to sit back and really look into our hearts.

Some people assume, "As long as I'm being a virgin, I'm being good." They compare themselves with others who are sleeping around on a regular basis, and as long as they see the world from that perspective, they feel like they are right on track. Meanwhile, they give away bits of themselves in passing relationships, all under the pretense that their friends are worse.

Do yourself a favor: Do not get technical about drawing a line at virginity, and saying that all else goes. If you can not decide if a particular action is "too far," imagine what the look on your future bride's or groom's face would be if you ever told her or him that you shared that act with another person. Make decisions now that would bless the heart of your future spouse, not wound it. (And *do not* be quick to discuss the specifics of your prior experience with potential spouses; a lot of that information could do *far* more harm than good.)

So where does the line go? For starters, know that the line begins in your mind. As soon as you begin to lust after a girl, stop. In regards to physical lines, an easy guideline to remember is, "Don't touch what you don't got." Also, I recommend no passionate kissing, kissing below the chin, or lying down together. That may seem extreme to some, but the more you become sensual and physical in a relationship, the more the relationship begins to revolve around that.

I will admit that this sounds a lot like "no," "no," "no," and "no," but think of it like this. There is a highway in California that runs up the coast. It is a gorgeous ride that takes you along the side of a sheer cliff that drops hundreds of feet to the ocean. Imagine that you were cruising along in your priceless sports car, and the passenger with you remarked, "Man, there is another one of those stupid guardrails. And look, another sign saying there is a sharp turn ahead. I hate how the California highway system inhibits your freedom, and tells you what to do." Odds are, you would not let the guy drive your car.

When we hear different moral laws about our sexuality, they are there for the same reason that guardrails and signposts mark a person's drive along the Pacific Coast Highway. If you want to express your freedom as you drive off the cliff, you are free to do so. But the purity of your soul is worth much more than a car. The Church's moral laws are there for our sake, so that we do not fall for counterfeit versions of love.

If you have tried everything else for years, try purity. You will not regret it. Each year I speak to over one hundred thousand teens about dating, sex, and relationships, and I have never met one who regretted what he or she did *not* do with a date. I have never had a high school girl come up to me in tears after a chastity talk because she did *not* sleep with her boyfriend. I have never had a guy confide in me that he was scared to death that his girlfriend was *not* pregnant. They regret what they have done, not what they have saved.

Imagine you were dating a beautiful young woman who you hoped to marry, and she had never kissed anyone because she wanted only her husband to know the touch of her lips. What man would not be flattered by her integrity and purity? What man would send her away to go a little further with the other guys? If we would be so honored by her, why would we not want to make a woman feel honored in the same way?

51

Can a girl get pregnant the first time? What if you do not go all the way with her?

Yes and yes. It is a myth that you can not get pregnant the first time, and many babies are living proof that the theory is wrong.

What most people do not know is that you can even get pregnant while remaining a virgin. Many teens engage in foreplay as a supposedly safe alternative to sex, but I know of a girl who is pregnant as I write this, and her doctors have confirmed that she is physiologically still a virgin. If any of the male's semen is released in the vicinity of the woman's genital area, she can become pregnant even if intercourse never took place.

If I am with a young woman and I am afraid that she might become pregnant, why am I afraid? If love by its very nature is life-giving, why would I live in fear? The reason is because my actions do not conform to love, and I know it. Love would never put a woman in the situation of having to deal with pregnancy outside of marriage.

52

My girlfriend and I have decided not to have sex. Is it wrong to sleep in the same bed occasionally?

It is understandable that a couple would want to lie down together. This is a natural desire. After all, who would not want to wake up next to their loved one? However, this kind of intimacy belongs only in marriage. To lie down with a woman in bed is marital. When we use the expression, "They slept together," we usually are not thinking about sleep at all. But this phrase is used because the marital act is inseparable from the marriage bed. In Hebrews 13:4, we are told to keep the marriage bed undefiled. It is to be sacred, and this means it is to be set apart for holy use. The holy use that God has in mind is marital union. In your heart you know that this belongs in marriage, because if you knew that sleeping in the same bed with her was pleasing to God, you would not have asked this question.

If you want to save sex for marriage, sleeping in the same bed is not the best way to guard that commitment. Granted, you may not be having sex, but as Proverbs 16:18 says, pride goes before a fall. There is wisdom in avoiding occasions of sin and not trusting ourselves too much. Promise each other that the next time the two of you share a bed, it will be as husband and wife. There is a time and a season for everything under the sun, and as difficult as this may be, purity calls you to make this sacrifice. After all, if the Lord calls you to marry her, you will have the rest of your life to fall asleep looking at her. But if you are not called to marry her, your future wife may not be thrilled to hear that you slept with another woman, even if you did not have a sexual relationship.

5

Pornography and Masturbation

53

What is wrong with looking at pornography? It's not like you are getting a girl pregnant or spreading STDs.

When Jesus warned that anyone who looks lustfully at a woman commits sin with her in his heart (Matt. 5:28), he spelled it out in no uncertain terms that it is not enough to avoid pregnancy or STDs. It is not even enough to avoid impure sexual contact; we must also resist impure sexual thoughts and looks.

The problem with using pornography, like indulging lust in any other way, is that it emasculates men, degrades women, destroys marriages, and offends the Lord. You may be thinking: "That's going a little overboard, don't you think? I mean, what's wrong with checking out a few Internet sites?" Take a look at the effects of pornography, and you will see why real men do not use it.

What does pornography do to a man? For starters, it robs him of the capacity to be a man. The essence of manhood consists in readiness to deny oneself for the good of a beloved. This is why Paul reminds husbands in his Letter to the Ephesians that their love must be like that of Christ, who allowed himself to be crucified for the sake of his beloved, the Church (Eph. 5:21–33).

Pornography defeats this calling. Instead of denying himself for the good of the woman, a man, through the use of porn, denies the woman her dignity in order to satisfy his lust. In essence, pornography is a rejection of our calling to love as God loves. It is no wonder that those who use it are never satisfied. Only love satisfies. Pornography fosters irresponsibility and degradation. (Ask yourself: Wouldn't it infuriate you if a guy looked at your daughter or wife in the same way he looked at pornography?)

Pornography gradually cripples a man's ability to love. It is impossible to love a fantasy, but living in a world of fantasy allows a guy to escape from reality and evade the demands of authentic love. In a way, the fact that pornography allows men to indulge their lust without having to worry about pregnancy or STDs is part of the *problem*. It encourages him to live in a world in which sexuality offers only pleasure without meaning or consequences, in which "no one gets pregnant, no one catches a disease, no one shows signs of guilt, fear, remorse, embarrassment, or distrust. No one suffers from the sexual activities of others and the men, at least, are always carefree, unrestrained. . . . The priority of lovingly protecting one's partner is of little concern in pornography because no harm seems possible." [99]

In the final analysis, pornography is the renunciation of love. As the writer Christopher West said, "[Pornography] seeks to foster precisely those distortions of our sexual desires that we must struggle *against* in order to discover true love." [100] For the person who indulges in porn, the purpose of sex becomes the satisfaction of the erotic "needs," not the communication of life and love. Pornography drives a man to value a woman only for what she gives him rather than for the person she is.

Some guys will slough this all off, saying, "Boys will be boys," or "I'm just appreciating the beauty of womanhood," or "I like the articles in the magazine." Sometimes they will realize how unconvincing these arguments are, and they will become resentful, saying, "You want to repress sexuality and rob women of their freedom. It is unhealthy for you to have such little appreciation for women!" This defensive attitude is apparent in the way strip clubs advertise themselves as "gentlemen's clubs" for "adult entertainment." Why would a man feel the need to justify his behavior as "gentlemanly" or "adult"? A man does not need to announce that he is a gentleman nor do adults need to remind others that they are mature. Actions speak for themselves.

Yet even when a man's lack of self-control makes him childish and his behavior cannot be reconciled with the title "gentleman," he still feels a need to identify with authentic manhood. No matter how far we fall, Christ has still stamped into our being the call to love as he loves. If we untwist the lies and humbly come before the Lord in our woundedness, he will raise us up and make us true men.

Now what does pornography do to women? Since it trains men to think of women as objects to be used instead of persons to be loved, guys speak of them as objects and treat them as objects. When men learn their "love" from videos and magazines, they accept the idea that a woman's "no" is actually a "yes" and that she enjoys being used. This can lead to a rapist mentality.

Consider, for example, a study done in the Oklahoma City area. When 150 sexually oriented businesses were closed, the rate of rape decreased 27 percent in five years, while the rate in the rest of the country increased 19 percent. In Phoenix, Arizona, neighborhoods with porn outlets had 500 percent more sex offenses than neighborhoods without them.[101]

Ted Bundy raped and killed dozens of women. He was sentenced to die in the electric chair and requested that his last interview be with Dr. James Dobson, the founder of Focus on the Family. In that meeting, Bundy talked only about pornography and told Dr. Dobson that his struggles all began there. He explained that an obsession with pornography gripped all of his fellow inmates who were motivated to violence as he was. Porn magazines and videos lay at the root of innumerable rapes and murders. No one can tell the husbands, siblings, children, and fathers of those violated and deceased women that pornography is harmless.

What does pornography do to marriages? To be blunt, pornography is the perfect way to shoot your future marriage in the head. Imagine that a young man has a habit of using pornography, and he does not reveal this to his fiancée. He hopes that once he is married, the desires for illicit sexual arousal will subside. But what becomes of his lust once he marries her? It does not disappear, it is foisted upon his wife. The pornography has trained him to react to the sexual value of a woman, and nothing else. He has trained himself to believe that women should be physically flawless and constantly sexually accessible. Even if he rejects this intellectually, the fact remains that his *attractions and responses* have been conditioned and shaped by warped, pornography-inspired fantasies.

Provided his wife is a life-size Barbie doll with a squad of make-up artists and hairdressers that follow her around the house, things might run smoothly for a time. But when reality confronts fantasy, the man will be left disillusioned and the woman's self image will suffer. His disordered desires and fantasies can never be fulfilled by any real-life woman. They focus solely upon self-centered gratification rather than mutual self-giving and joy in pleasing one's spouse. One woman explained that if a man's real-life partner is not always as available sexually and willing to do whatever he wishes as the women he has fantasized about, he may accuse her of being a prude. If she looks normal, and unlike the models he has come to adore, he may accuse her of being fat. If she has needs, unlike the passive images in the magazines, then she may seem too demanding for him. [102]

In other words, he will be quick to blame his disorder on her; his fantasies will have robbed him of the ability to be truly intimate with his wife. One reason he is unable to have healthy intimacy with his wife is because intimacy is not an escape from reality, but the capacity to see the beauty of the other. The presence of lust in the heart of the man blocks his ability to view the woman as a person. He has reduced her to an object and ignored her value as person. When this happens, he forfeits love. True intimacy is impossible.

This is why part of the problem with pornography is not simply that it shows too much, but that it shows too little. It reduces a woman to nothing more than her body. Thus, a man will assume that the greater the body, the greater the value of the woman. With this mindset, men not only expect their future wives to look no less perfect than Miss September, they also do not appreciate a woman's most beautiful and precious qualities, since a centerfold display fails to highlight these. This drives men to look elsewhere in an impossible quest to satisfy their disordered appetites. After all, pornography fosters the false mentality that casual, uncommitted sex is the most fulfilling and enjoyable. Who does not want to be fulfilled?

One all-too-common response to the marital dissatisfaction often caused by pornography habits is to actually bring pornography into the bedroom. This is a vain effort on the part of the man to have the illicit excitement that he has formed an attachment to. The poor wife may allow this, but the joy of loving has escaped the man, who no longer sees the value of the person and the need to give himself for her. Married couples who use pornography find that their marital problems only worsen. If a husband needs to pretend that his wife is someone else in order for him to be excited, then he will become less and less drawn to her. Instead of making love to her, he is destroying love between them.

Because the effects of pornography are so severe, Christian men have an obligation to rid their own lives of it. According to Pope John Paul II, "[God] has assigned as a duty to every man the dignity of every woman." [103] When we act in a way that is contrary to the dignity of women, we act contrary to our own dignity and vocation as men. For this reason, the Holy Father says, "Each man must look within himself to see whether she who was entrusted to him as a sister in humanity, as a spouse, has not become in his heart an object of adultery." [104]

Even if pornography had no adverse affects on people, we must never forget that sin is not simply a social matter. We owe it to our neighbor to love him, but we also owe it to God to honor the Lord in all our actions and thoughts. To lust after his daughters is a grave sin, even if no one becomes pregnant as a result of another's imagination. "So shun youthful passions and aim at righteousness, faith, love, and peace, along with those who call upon the Lord from a pure heart" (2 Tim. 2:22).

54

I have been looking at porn on the Internet for years, and I am finding it practically impossible to overcome the habit. How do I finally rid myself of the stuff?

Be assured that where sin abounds, grace abounds all the more (Rom. 5:20). I recommend four steps that will help you resist the temptation in the future. First, you must become a man of prayer. Prayer is essential for those who want to persevere in purity (this applies to women as well). In particular, go to Mass often, receive the sacrament of reconciliation whenever you fall, and develop a strong devotion to the rosary and to St. Joseph. This is pretty much a one-two-three punch for fighting temptations to indulge illicit desires.

Second, do whatever you can to rid yourself of occasions of sin. If you have pornographic magazines or videos, throw them all away immediately. Since the Internet has been a problem, at the very least you should install filtering software on your computer. You might even want to consider whether there is any way you can take a break from using the web entirely, or go awhile with minimal web access (perhaps with the images turned off in your browser or with a text-only browser, like Lynx, that does not use images). Also, visit some of the web sites in the resource section of this book that can help you overcome the temptations. Another useful strategy is to put holy objects and pictures wherever you had the images. If it is on the Internet, put a crucifix or picture of our Lady on top of the computer, and have a sacred image for your screen saver or computer wallpaper.

Third, find a person with whom you can be honest about your habit, and be accountable to him. A priest, family member, youth minister, or good friend should be able to help you win the battle. As the Bible says, "Two are better than one. . . . If they fall, one will lift up his fellow; but woe to him who is alone when he falls and has not another to lift him up. . . . And though a man might prevail against one who is alone, two will withstand him. A threefold cord is not quickly broken" (Eccles. 4:9–12).

Fourth, take a look at your motivation to overcome the habit. Are you simply trying to conquer the temptations because the habit is embarrassing, or because you are afraid you will be caught? Elevate your motivation so that you are working to overcome the problem for the sake of love. Do it for the love of God and to make yourself a fit person for your future bride.

When a person looks at pornography, on some level he is looking for love. It is a warped attempt to give of yourself and receive another. The fantasy woman may seem like she is entirely yours, although a million other men feel the same way toward her. It is obviously a false oneness, and we must refuse it in order to obtain the greater good that awaits us. If a young man longs for love, then he must strive to acquire the selflessness that will enable him to properly love a woman. Getting rid of porn should not be seen as a loss but as an opportunity to grow in that selflessness.

Imagine that you found the woman of your dreams and got married. As you carry her across the threshold of your honeymoon suite, she wraps her arms around your neck, looks into your eyes and whispers how excited she is. She tells you that she has waited all her life for this day, and to make it extra special, she has been looking at thousands of pornographic images of men on the Internet. You would probably drop her on the floor. You see, not only should we wait for our spouses with our bodies, we must wait for them with our minds. So for the sake of love, trash the pornographic magazines, web sites, and videos. If you are called to the sacrament of marriage, isn't your bride worth waiting to see, instead of filling your mind with images of other women's bodies?

55

I threw away all my pornography a long time ago, but how do you clear your head of all the images stamped into it? I go to confession and Mass and I pray regularly, but I feel like they are branded in there.

I know of a high school student who said, "Every time I get an impure thought, I try to think about Ross Perot, and it goes away." While this is amusing, it is only a coping mechanism. It may sweep the bad thought under the rug, but it does not deal with it.

Here is one strategy for handling it: Every time one of those impure images pops into your mind, take that as an occasion to pray for that woman's conversion.

Pray specifically for her, and lift her to Jesus. This makes up for the times you have lusted after her but will accomplish even more. If you persevere in this practice, I would imagine that the thoughts subside considerably. Stay strong, because resisting these temptations will foster in you the virtues that make for great dads and husbands.

Other than this, continue with your prayer life and remain pure in your day-to-day relationships. And finally, deepen your devotion to Mary. We need to have our image of womanhood redeemed, and praying a daily rosary is an ideal way to begin this reconstruction. The remedy for pornography is to understand the dignity of womanhood and the truth about your call to love. Then, and only then, will the pornography be seen for what it is—a sham.

You can and will lose the desire to look at pornography. You will not lose sexual desire, but when you see women degraded, you will be filled with pity for them instead of lust. In the words of C. S. Lewis, "Lust is a weak, poor, whimpering whispering thing when compared with that richness and energy of desire which will arise when lust has been killed." [105] Only when you empty yourself for the good of a beloved will you see that all other joy is an illusion.

56

What is wrong with masturbation? I think of it as getting rid of your temptations without leading anyone into sin.

Masturbation does not "get rid of" temptations any more than a prostitute does. Both may temporarily relieve sexual desires, but our goal as Christians is not simply to get rid of temptations, but to glorify God with our bodies. The idea that masturbation can be used to decrease sexual desires is like saying that lighter fluid can be used to extinguish a fire. If anything, masturbation incites lustful thoughts and teaches a person that he or she deserves— and needs—sexual gratification whenever the desire arises.

To understand why masturbation is wrong, we need to step back from the world's constant clamoring for sexual "needs" and go back to God's plan for sex. Sexuality is meant to be a gift between a husband and wife for the purpose of babies and bonding. When it is taken out of that context the gift is degraded—and in the case of masturbation, altogether ceases being a gift. The purpose of sexuality is abandoned, because the center of the sexual act becomes "me" instead of "we" and the person is trained to look to himself for sexual fulfillment. The gift of one's sexuality is misused for the sake of lifeless pleasure. Only selfless giving will fulfill you.

When people misuse their sexuality in this way, they begin to use pleasure to change their mood, release tension, or forget their loneliness. Masturbation becomes an escape. It may pacify them, but it will never satisfy them, because they will always want more. They use the fantasies of their mind and the pleasures of their body to flee from reality and the call to love. Their goal in sexual activity has been reduced to merely receiving pleasure instead of showing love. If men and women have trained themselves to use their sexuality in this way, why would this suddenly change once they are married? The husband or wife will simply be a substitute for the fantasies, to be used in place of self. They may even imagine the fantasies while with their spouse. The problem is that the lust will be transferred to the other, not healed within.

Worse yet, merely getting married will not cure their problem with masturbation. Because masturbation has trained disordered impulses in them, the true pleasures of marriage—though far superior—will not appease their warped attachments. Where will they turn to find those pleasures within marriage? Often, they will continue to struggle with masturbation, to the sorrow and distress of their spouse, and to the detriment of their marriage. A person who does not preserve his own purity when alone will have a difficult time remaining pure with another. If he lacks self-control when alone, he will be unable to properly give himself to his spouse when the time comes. You can not give what you do not control. No self-control equals no gift of self. To the extent that there is no gift of self, there is no love. If you want to be able to genuinely love your spouse, you must build self-mastery.

57

Someone at school said that it was unhealthy not to masturbate, and in the long run it could be harmful to your body if you don't. Is that true?

This is a myth. As far as a man is concerned, his prostate gland produces seminal fluid on a "need to" basis. There is not a constant buildup of pressure that will harm an individual unless he masturbates. The next time you hear a claim such as this, ask the person to show you the medical research to support what he is saying.

If anything, the scientific evidence seems to show that masturbation is harmful for both men and women. If you have ever taken a class in psychology, you probably learned about Pavlov's dog. Pavlov was a guy who rang a bell every time he was about to feed his dog. By doing this, the dog came to associate the bell with food, and would begin salivating at the sound of the bell. This is known as a trained response.

The human mind can be trained in the same way. In fact, the pleasure center of the brain is the most easily trained part of the human mind. This center is called the Medial Pre-optic Nucleus (MPN), and when the body experiences great pleasure, as in a sexual release, this part of the brain is rewarded. According to the research of Dr. Douglas Weiss,[106] when a person experiences sexual arousal, the brain releases endorphins that help train the MPN to associate pleasure with whatever the person is doing, looking at, smelling, and so on. Unconsciously, a person forms a bond between a particular image, scent, or person and the feeling of sexual pleasure.

This bond is further solidified by the release of a neuropeptide called oxytocin during sexual release. This also creates a bond between people during a sexual act. If a person is alone, it still creates a mental bond with whomever he is fantasizing about. The bonding mechanism is damaged through casual sex.[107] This scientific discovery sheds new light on Paul's words: "Do you not know that he who joins himself to a prostitute becomes one body with her? For, as it is written, 'The two shall become one flesh.' . . . Shun immorality. Every other sin which a man commits is outside the body; but the immoral man *sins against his own body*" (1 Cor. 6:16–18).

When a person experiences a sexual release while masturbating and lusting after another in his imagination, he is training his brain to be stimulated by fantasy images in his own mind. If this is what a man's or woman's brain identifies as the cause of sexual joy, then where does this leave his or her spouse one day? This is not a fantasy image, but a real human being. Yet instead of being able to take joy in the actual person in the marriage bed, the individual trained by masturbation may be driven to find stimulation in inner fantasies even while trying to make love to a spouse. Men and women may look to adultery, strip clubs, pornography, or a disordered lust for one another to satiate their desires. Often, especially for men, the habit of masturbation continues in order to take care of sexual "needs." This becomes a cancer in marriage.

Now, this does not mean that you are doomed to a dysfunctional marriage if you have ever experienced sexual pleasure with anyone other than your husband or wife. However, it does mean that you will have obstacles to overcome that those without such a history will not struggle with. The brain can be retrained, but it will take time according to how well-entrenched the habit of lust has become.

This should show us that God's plan for our sexuality is stamped into our anatomy. When people live according to God's truths, their bodies will associate sexual joy with their spouse. God has designed our bodies to ensure that a married couple will be physiologically drawn toward each other. Their minds have been trained that way. As the Bible says, "Let [your springs] be for yourself alone, and not for strangers with you. Let your fountain be blessed, and rejoice in the wife of your youth, a lovely hind, a graceful doe. Let her affection fill you at all times with delight, be infatuated always with her love" (Prov. 5:17–19).

58

I have formed a real habit of masturbation and do not know how to stop. What would you say is the best way to overcome this?

Prayer and patient perseverance. As you begin the battle, know that God is pleased with your desire for holiness and that his grace is working in your life. He will complete the good work he has begun in you (Phil. 1:6). Come to him in prayer and ask him often for the grace to be pure, and specifically to overcome this habit. The number one prayer you can offer is the holy sacrifice of the Mass. There is enough grace in one Communion to make you a saint. Tap into that fountain of purity!

Spend an increased amount of time in personal prayer as well, and speak openly to Jesus about your struggles. Also, pray the Hail Mary three times each day for purity of mind, body, and heart;

frequent the sacrament of reconciliation; read Scripture; pray the rosary; make the Stations of the Cross; and develop a devotion to St. Joseph. These form an arsenal of weapons against any sin. Use them often, and you will either stop the sin or you will stop these prayers and good habits. They cannot last long together.

If you need to confess the same sin repeatedly, do so. The devil will try to discourage you, saying, "Hey, you've been back in the confessional so many times with this sin. Why don't you give up? You can't win." Recognize these thoughts as a temptation and turn immediately to prayer. Know that the patient is healed who shows his wound to the physician. The confessional is the medicine box, Christ in the priest is the doctor, and that is the last place the devil wants you to be. You are on the winning team, and the Lord will not let you be snatched from his hand. You can not do it alone, but you can do all things through Christ who gives you strength (Phil. 4:13).

Certainly, if you own any pornography, swimsuit posters, vulgar music and such, get rid of them immediately. For the sake of love, guard yourself against such contamination. Replace these things with good Christian music and put holy images in your room, especially where you usually fall into the sin. If you have a habit of watching a lot of television, find something else to do, such as exercise. This helps release tension and makes the body easier to master. Television is idleness filled with temptation, and that is kindling for the fires of lust.

To help you grow in discipline, set reachable goals. For example, make a commitment not to masturbate for three days, a week, a month, or whatever you feel is a reasonable time. When you have made it to that point, you will have an increased sense of confidence that you do have control over your body. Then, bump up the time and abstain for a longer period. Keep this up until the vice is overcome.

During this time of discipline, give up tiny things. For example, skip salt on your fries, or skip seconds at a meal. These small sacrifices will help you grow in self-mastery, so that you gain self-control. After all, we are slaves to whatever rules us. The difference is like that between a jockey who has no control over his horse which gallops wildly through gardens and living rooms, and a jockey who has control and can win races and stop on a dime. That is a person fully alive. This kind of self-control is impossible alone, but with the grace of God, all things are possible. If you ask for purity, not one grace will be lacking. Be patient with yourself and do not give in to discouragement. According to the Gospel of Luke, "By your endurance you will gain your lives" (Luke 21:19). The prize of true love awaits those that are truly free, because they are the only ones capable of giving and receiving.

6

Homosexuality

59

If two people of the same sex really love each other and are willing to stay faithful for life, why can't they get married?

The reason why people of the same sex who love each other and are willing to be faithful for life can not get married is because there is more to marriage than love and faithfulness. These are necessary ingredients, but they are not the only ones. Our modern culture finds it difficult to understand why marriage is only for heterosexuals because it does not understand marriage itself. This difficulty exists partly because contraception has divorced procreation from sex and marriage. If a heterosexual couple can have intercourse without the possibility of pregnancy, why can't members of the same sex have intercourse?

To understand why marriage is only for the joining of a man and a woman, we need to step back from the influences of the world and define the essential characteristics of marriage and sex. We did not invent either one. They are God's creation, and he has ordained marriage and sexual union to be free, total, faithful, and open to life. Although a same-sex couple may be able to freely choose an exclusive and lifelong relationship with one another, they are unable to have the kind of sexual relations that could ever be open to life. Imagine a couple who agreed to marry and have children, but who refused on the day of their wedding to commit to being faithful to one another. This is not a marriage. Likewise, two members of the same sex are unable to have the kind of union that could ever be open to life. Therefore, they cannot have a marriage—let alone a true union.

Although same-sex temptations, like temptations in general, are not in and of themselves sinful, Scripture and Church teaching condemn homosexual actions (Rom. 1:24–27, Gen. 19:1–29, 1 Tim. 1:8–10, CCC 2357–2359). So, if two members of the same sex are mutually attracted, and they really love one another, they will do everything necessary to do what is best for each other. They desire union because of their love, but love desires more than a temporary physical union; it desires the good of the other. It desires heaven for that person and will encourage him to embrace the call to chastity.

60

What causes homosexuality? If it is genetic, is it okay to be gay if you are born that way?

The causes of homosexuality are not fully understood, and many people who struggle with the temptations do not choose or want them. There has been much debate over the issue of nature versus nurture, but scientists have been unable to find a genetic cause for homosexuality. Dr. Dean Hamer (who coined the phrase "gay gene") said, "We have not found the gene—which we don't think exists—for sexual orientation." [108] Another recent study concluded, "Critical review shows the evidence favoring a biologic (genetic) theory to be lacking." [109]

There may be genetic factors that have yet to be discovered, but the development of homosexual desires often appears rooted in an individual's upbringing. [110] In my research and ministry, I have frequently encountered the following four issues related to the onset of homosexual attractions.

One: The same-sex parent was often emotionally or physically absent in the home of those who struggle with homosexuality. In the case of a young man, the absence of a father may lead to feelings of inferiority or rejection by peers when it comes to athletic endeavors with the other guys.

Two: Sometimes a parent is sexually abusive. If a father (or another male) abuses a girl, she may subconsciously think, "Men must all be like you, and no man will do that to me! I don't want to be hurt that way again." At times, homosexuality becomes a shield for the heart and a sort of haven to escape the hurt of abusive relationships. It is understandable that a person hurt in the past would want to avoid future relationships that cause pain—and pain is all a person may know from the opposite sex. Also, a child who was sexually abused by a member of the same sex can become confused about his or her sexual orientation.

Three: Sometime the opposite-sex parent is too enmeshed in the life of the child. For example, a mother and son can rely too exclusively on one another for needs that should be met elsewhere. This can contribute to gender identity confusion in the child.

Four: It is common that as a young man matures he will seek to identify with what is masculine. Sometimes this desire to identify with a guy who is particularly masculine may be confused with the onset of homosexuality. If a young man acts on this and begins to explore homosexuality, he may gradually come to believe that his orientation is homosexual. But the attraction may have been there simply because the other guy possessed a masculinity that the young man admired and feared that he lacked.

This admiration of a member of the same sex is not uncommon during adolescence, for women as well as men. During this time, young people are trying to discover who they are. They often go through a maturing process that moves them from a strong interest in same-sex friendships to a primary interest in opposite-sex relationships. It is not unusual for adolescents to feel confusion in the midst of their rapid sexual development, identity search, and maturing of interests.

Let us assume for the sake of argument that people are born homosexual and that is their orientation. Does this mean they should be free to indulge in homosexual behavior? As a young man, I could claim that I am genetically wired to desire premarital sex. Some men claim to be disposed toward incest or child molestation. But just because a person has certain desires, this does not mean that it is moral to act on those urges.

61

Recently I have been feeling attraction for some other guys at my high school. I have not told anyone yet because I do not even understand what's going on in me. I love God, but I am scared and I do not know what to do. Any advice?

Do not be afraid. Your temptations do not affect God's love for you. During the high school years, the body develops rapidly, spurred on by profound hormonal changes. Because of this, teens are often at a loss to understand all of the feelings they experience. Even if a feeling of attraction persists for some time, this does not mean that it will be permanent. I know of many men who were actively homosexual but left that lifestyle and created successful marriages and families. Just because you have feelings that you are unable to explain, this does not mean that God is unhappy with you or that you are incapable of living a fulfilled heterosexual life.

Let us assume, though, that the attractions and even temptations do not subside. I have friends who have homosexual temptations, but I do not speak of them as "gay" or even as "homosexuals." To do so would be to define them by a label, as if that is all there is to them, and that is all they will ever be. We should not define ourselves by our struggles. "Homosexual" is not what you are. For one thing, you are a guy with many talents, struggles, gifts, and other characteristics, but most important of all, you are a son of God, and *that* is your identity. Therefore, do not identify yourself with your brokenness but with your calling.

One day, during an interview, someone asked Mother Teresa for her views on homosexuality. She announced that she did not like the word *homosexual*. She stopped the interview and told the reporters that if they had any more questions about homosexuals, they would refer to them from now on as "Friends of Jesus." This is how the Church sees those who carry this cross.

It might help to know that you are not alone in what you are experiencing. Look in the resource section at the back of this book for the contact information for a group called *Courage*. This is the best movement for those who struggle with homosexuality and want to glorify God with their lives. Another group, the National Association for Research and Therapy of Homosexuality (NARTH) might also prove helpful (see resource section). Sometimes a person struggling with homosexuality can benefit from counseling rooted in a Catholic perspective. NARTH can help direct people to such counselors.

I am sure this is all frightening for you and you may feel alone. You are not alone. A large fellowship of men and women is growing closer to God while carrying this same cross and persisting in the virtue of chastity. In the meantime, come to God in prayer to be loved by him as you are. He will help you do the rest.

62

I go to an all-guys school, and my friends and I sometimes make fun of effeminate guys. Is that wrong?

Yes. In fact, it is a sign of male insecurity for a guy to tear down other men in order to establish his masculinity. A real man is able to love those who struggle with homosexuality. I went to an all-guys high school as well, and I took part in mocking guys who were effeminate. Our jokes, mannerisms, and voice impersonations were a constant announcement to the world that none of us understood manhood yet. Lurking under the mockery, though, was the knowledge that we would be scared to death if any of us had to carry that cross.

In the future, refuse to take part in such behavior. Whatever we have done to another, we have done to Christ himself (Matt. 25:31–46).

7

Contraception

63

Why doesn't the Catholic Church allow married couples to use contraception?

Contraception is nothing new; history records people using various methods of artificial birth control four thousand years ago. Ancient people swallowed potions to cause temporary sterility; they used linens, wool, or animal skins as barrier methods; they fumigated the uterus with poison to keep it from bearing life. The Romans practiced contraception but the early Christians stood out from the pagan culture because they refused to use it.[111] Scripture condemned the act (Gen. 38:8-10), as did all Christian denominations before 1930. At that time, the Anglican church decided to allow contraception in some circumstances. They soon gave in on the issue altogether and, before long, all Protestant denominations followed suit. Now only the Catholic Church stands fast on the teaching of historic Christianity. But why? Why does not the Church "get with the times"?

The modern world has trouble understanding the Church's stance on contraception because the world does not know the purpose of sex. The writer Frank Sheed said that "Modern man practically never thinks about sex." He dreams of it, craves it, pictures it, drools over it, but never pauses to actually *think* about it. Sheed continued: "Our typical modern man, when he gives his mind to it at all, thinks of sex as something we are lucky enough to have; and he sees all its problems rolled into the one problem of how to get the most pleasure out of it."[112]

But we should put more thought into the matter. Who invented sex? What is sex? What is its purpose? What is it worth?

For starters, God invented sex. Since he is its author, he knows its meaning and purpose better than we do. God has revealed that the purposes of sex are procreation and union (babies and bonding), and that the sexual act can be thought of as the wedding vows made flesh. The wedding vows are promises that your love will be *free, faithful, total,* and *open to life.* Each act of marital intercourse should be a renewal of these vows.

Some couples say that they will be *open to life,* but in the meantime they will contracept. In other words, they will be completely open to life . . . except when they sterilize their acts of love. Imagine if they had the same mentality with other parts of the wedding vows. Can a husband say the marital act is free even if he forces himself upon his wife? No, she must be able to *freely* offer the gift of self. Can he say that he will give himself *totally* to his bride even though he refuses to give her the gift of his fertility and wants nothing to do with her fertility? No. He must make a total gift of self. Or can a wife say she is *faithful* because 99 percent of the time she has intercourse with her husband and rarely sleeps with other men? This is obviously absurd, but contracepting couples turn away from their vows to be open to God's gift of life. When it comes down to it, they are afraid of what sex really means.

But sex is more than the wedding vows made flesh. It is also a reflection of the life-giving love of the Trinity. In the words of Carlo Cardinal Martini, "In the Bible, the man-woman couple is not meant to be simply a preservation of the species, as is the case for the other animals. Insofar as it was called to become the image and likeness of God, it expresses in a bodily, tangible way the face of God, which is Love." [113] God's plan for us to love as he loves is stamped into our very being, and so there is really only one question to ask when it comes to sexual morality: "Am I expressing God's love through my body?" When a married couple does this, they become what they are—an image of trinitarian love—and through this they unveil the love of God to the world.

The act of life-giving love between a husband and wife is also meant to be a mirror of the love that Christ has for his Church. We should ask ourselves: "If we consider the relationship between

Christ and his Church, where does contraception fit into the picture? What is contraceptive about Christ's love?"

Beyond the theological implications, consider the consequences of contraception in society. When contraception spread among Christians, the Catholic Church warned about the harm it would inflict on relationships. Rates of marital infidelity would rise because spouses could be unfaithful without fear of pregnancy. Since contraception offers an easy way to elude the moral law, there would be a general lowering of morality. The Church "feared that the man, growing used to the employment of anti-conceptive practices, may finally lose respect for the woman, and no longer caring for her physical and psychological equilibrium, may come to the point of considering her a mere instrument of selfish enjoyment, and no longer as his respected and beloved companion."[114] Furthermore, if people could separate making love from making life, then why would those acts that are unable to make life (homosexual sex or masturbation) be forbidden? Sex would lose its deepest meaning and the clear sign of God's love would be lost.

The Church did not hesitate to point out the vast implications of contraception. Anthropologists who study the origin and destruction of civilizations point out that societies that do not direct their sexual energies toward the good of marriage and family begin to crumble.[115]

The love between a husband and wife holds a marriage together. A strong marriage holds the family together. Strong families hold society together, and a civilization will stand or fall upon this. "The future of humanity," according to the Church, "passes by way of the family."[116] If it can be shown that contraception compromises intimacy between a husband and wife, invites selfishness into the marital act, and opens a door for greater infidelity, then contraception is a cancer within civilization.

64

If the Church forbids contraception, does it expect married women to have fifteen kids?

Although the Church is opposed to contraception, it is not opposed to the responsible regulation of births. Couples may use Natural Family Planning (NFP) to do this, if they have a just reason to do so.

NFP is a method of spacing births that can be more effective than contraception.[117] Since a woman can conceive only three to five days each month, a couple who is practicing NFP will refrain from marital relations when the woman has a chance of conceiving. This method is often confused with the outdated calendar "rhythm method," but in reality it is very different. With an effectiveness rate of 99 percent, NFP is far more reliable.[118] NFP is also an effective means to achieve pregnancy, since the couple has a deep understanding of the woman's fertility. And by monitoring the woman's fertility, they are more aware of reproductive abnormalities that may need treatment.

Many people think that the Church's opposition to contraception is an attack on the freedom of women to have control over their bodies. Nothing could be further from the truth. The Church insists that we have control over our bodies (CCC 2339). By having control over one's body, a person is able to make a gift of one's self.

The contraception industry would like its customers to believe that contraception grants them control over their bodies, relationships, and sex lives. While contraception offers a person license —the ability to live without responsibility—that is not freedom. Freedom can only be attained through self-control. Some people use birth control to make up for their lack of self-control. Thus, they never experience genuine freedom.

Contraception can never make woman free. To treat pregnancy as if it were a disease implies that there is something defective in the way she was created—that her fertility is a curse. That is not a very liberating experience for any woman. NFP is a beautiful alternative because it does not treat a woman's body as if it needs to be subdued by drugs or shielded behind barriers in order to function properly. It invites the man to treat the woman's fertility with reverence instead of disdain. This is true sexual liberation.

65

If couples are using NFP to space births, what is the difference between that and contraception?

There are four enormous differences between NFP and contraception. The first is the morality of the act; the second deals with the fact that some contraceptives work by causing abortions; the third issue pertains to adverse side effects that are caused by contraceptives; and the last issue deals with the fruits of NFP.

Suppose that a married couple is using contraceptives for the same reason another couple is practicing NFP. Both couples already have children and hope to have more. But for good reasons, they need to space the next birth by a couple of years. Both have the intent to regulate births, and responsible parenthood allows couples not to have more children than they can care for. However, the good intent of a couple is not sufficient to determine the morality of their act. By way of comparison, if two women wanted to avoid becoming overweight, one might go on a diet and the other might binge and purge (bulimia). Both may stay slim, but one succumbs to gluttony and unnatural, unhealthy behavior, while the other exercises the virtue of temperance.

Similarly, the Church's condemnation of contraception does not imply that the couple has bad intentions but that they are using a means that is immoral. Married couples are free to have intercourse (or to agree to abstain from it) on any given day, regardless of the wife's fertility. But when they do join as one flesh, they must not frustrate the purpose God designed that act to have. It is God alone who has the power to create an immortal soul as a result of the marital act and to contracept is to say that God's presence is not desired. Clearly then, a couple abstaining from sex for a just reason can not be compared to a couple who sterilizes their acts of lovemaking in order to enjoy the pleasure of the marital act apart from God's design.

The reason the Church denounces contraception is not because it is artificial. After all, the Church allows the use of countless artificial drugs and other technological advances that medicine can offer man. However, these are to be used to heal dysfunction and promote the proper functioning of the body as God ordained it. Contraception does the opposite: It *prevents* the natural functioning of the body.

Therefore, the moral difference between NFP and contraception is that contraception deliberately interrupts, sterilizes, and works against (*contra*) the marital act and the beginning of life, while NFP respects the way God ordained it to work. In no way does NFP interrupt or sterilize an act of intercourse. NFP couples are not acting against the way God has designed fertility, but are working with it.

Another major difference between NFP and contraceptives is that some birth control methods work by causing abortions. For example: the intrauterine device (IUD), Norplant, Depo-Provera, and the low-dose birth control pill often work by preventing a newly conceived child from attaching to the uterus. This causes a first trimester abortion to occur—without the mother even knowing it.

All contraceptives have potential adverse side effects, most of which affect the woman. Later in this chapter, I go into detail regarding the side effects of contraceptives. Here I will simply point out that depending on the method used, these may include a heightened risk of breast cancer, a greater risk of contracting a sexually transmitted disease, migraine headaches, high blood pressure, increased fetal abnormalities, and toxic shock syndrome.

Finally, consider the implications of the fact that *couples who use NFP have a divorce rate of 1 to 3 percent.*[119] In one study, there were zero divorces out of fourteen hundred NFP couples.[120] Keep in mind that more than half of all marriages end in divorce. The striking correlation between NFP and strong marriages is an important indication of the close relationship between NFP and the way God designed marriage and sex to work. This close correlation is explored in further detail below.

Also, NFP offers something else that contraceptives cannot: an understanding of how to time intercourse to achieve pregnancy. Further, NFP couples are in a much better position to teach their teens about sexual self-control. A couple should not expect their children to follow the Church's teachings on sexuality outside of marriage if they as parents are not willing to follow the Church's teachings on sexuality within marriage. When we consider the positive impact of NFP on a marriage and the potential dangers of contraception, the most loving option becomes obvious.

Despite all of these differences, NFP can be abused. Because it is so effective in regulating births, a couple could take on a contraceptive mentality and close themselves off from the gift of life. NFP must be practiced responsibly and only when there is just reason to do so.

66

Why do NFP couples have such low divorce rates?

The low divorce rate among couples practicing NFP reflects a combination of factors. First, couples with strong relationships are overwhelmingly more likely than other couples to choose to practice NFP. Second, NFP actually helps strengthen marital relationships. NFP depends on some of the same virtues as marriage itself —commitment, communication, consideration, and self-control. Couples who reject NFP as "too much trouble" or "too restrictive" all too often turn out to be the same couples who ultimately find the demands of marriage itself too much to handle.

It is difficult to count all the ways that NFP strengthens a marriage. On the most basic level, since the spouses are not constantly sexually available to the other, this keeps them from taking the other for granted. Often, women rightly complain that the use of contraception has lowered their sense of worth.

I recently received a letter from a woman who said that while she and her first husband were using contraception, she felt like a "toy or a recreational vehicle." The contraception made her husband assume that she was always sexually available, and she felt used and taken for granted. She has since been married in the Church and has used NFP for years. In her words, "a chaste marriage is the ultimate!" After abandoning contraception and switching to NFP, another woman said, "I now know the true meaning of the word 'intimate.' "[121]

When was the last time you heard a woman say that using a spermicide is "the ultimate!" and that after using a condom she finally knew the meaning of intimacy? The enthusiasm has never been there because no woman wants to be at war with her body. Sure, she may want to delay pregnancy, but she has never been ecstatic about the methods commonly offered to do that. She may seem content, but she silently wishes there was a better arrangement.

NFP is this better way, and couples who make the switch are more than pleased with the results. One way to measure a couple's satisfaction with a method of spacing births is to look at how many continue to use it over time. For example, as pointed out in the book *Love and Family,* spermicides have a 43 percent continuation rate, the diaphragm a 58 percent rate, the condom, 63 percent, and the Pill, 72 percent. What about NFP? Its continuation rate is higher than any form of contraception—93 percent.[122]

The Church explains that the practice of NFP "favors attention for one's partner, helps both parties to drive out selfishness, the enemy of true love, and deepens their sense of responsibility."[123] Many men do not realize that there is a time for a wife to be touched and held, and a time for her to be free from embraces. Men who sacrifice to give a woman that space improve the unity and intimacy of the marriage. The relationship has space to breathe. In the words of one husband, "It's wonderful because it almost creates the honeymoon over and over again."[124] During the times of abstinence, the spouses learn to express love in non-sexual ways. As a result, the intimacy between them deepens. In the meantime, their anticipation of the marital act will also intensify its joy. Furthermore, even the act of abstaining from intercourse can be a loving gesture, since not having more children at that time may be best for the family.

At times, couples resort to sex as a way to solve problems when in reality they are only burying the issues under a false sense of closeness. Since complete physical intimacy is not always possible for the couple practicing NFP, they cannot as easily use the feeling of physical intimacy to cover up conflicts. This opens a door for them to deepen their ability to communicate and solve problems. As a result, their exchange of the marital act is not as likely to be a means to bury problems, but will be seen as an opportunity to celebrate their love.

Also the use of contraception fosters a level of rejection between spouses. By sterilizing the act of intercourse, the woman is saying that she wants to make love, but will kill any sperm that come her way.[125] The man is saying that he accepts everything about the woman except for her womb. He gives everything to her except his potential fatherhood. The language of sex should be that of complete self-donation, but that is impossible with contraception. Since the body reveals the person, a rejection of the body is a rejection of the spouse.

Also, couples who reject contraception generally do not see pregnancy as a disease, or children as a burden. Because of their generous spirit, they tend to have larger families, and divorce rates are highest where children are fewest. NFP couples also tend to take their faith, and therefore the sacrament of marriage, more seriously than the average contracepting couple. Lastly, since the couple never sterilizes acts of intercourse, they are truly renewing their wedding vows each time they exchange the marital act. Knowing that they are not blocking God's plan for life and love, their times of unity as one flesh take on the joy, peace, and freedom that come from obeying the Lord, and his bride, the Church.

67

Isn't contraceptive sex better than spreading disease and having un-wanted teen pregnancies and abortions?

We should look at each of these issues and see if contraception is part of the solution . . . or part of the problem.

In regard to the spread of disease, it is important to remember that contraception was not created to prevent infections, but to prevent pregnancies. In fact, some forms of contraception harm the immune system, making the user more likely to contract certain STDs. [126]

According to the latest research, the evidence is insufficient to show that the condom provides protection against many of the most common STDs. [127] Yet the contraception industry perpetuates the misconception that condoms make sex safe, thus encouraging teens and others to engage in risky behavior under a false sense of security. Those who favor the distribution of condoms have always promised that this would decrease the prevalence of STDs. The opposite has happened.

The same is true of unwanted pregnancies. [128] With the spread of contraception, more people than ever have sex without wanting children. Sex out of wedlock has become far more common, and more sex means more babies. Some argue that teaching people how to use contraceptives properly will alleviate the problem. But research shows that "programs in safer sex education and condom distribution have not reduced the out-of-wedlock birthrates among sexually experienced teens. . . . The fact is, increased condom use by teens is associated with *increased* out-of-wedlock birth rates." [129] A few years ago in Colorado, one school began passing out condoms to the students. Within three years, the birth rate rose 31 percent above the national average, and in one school year they were expecting one hundred births out of the twelve hundred students. The administrators were described as "searching for explanations." [130]

When unwanted pregnancies occur, many turn to abortion as

a solution. They feel that the "fault" of the pregnancy can be blamed on the failed contraception, but by contracepting, they have already set their wills against new life. Since contraception treats pregnancy as if it were a disease, many people conclude that abortion must be the cure. I once saw a condom advertisement that called pregnancy "the mother of all nightmares." With this mentality, it is no surprise that the sex researcher Alfred Kinsey said "We have found the highest frequency of induced abortion in the group which, in general, most frequently used contraceptives."[131] Studies also reveal that the provision of contraception leads to an increase in the abortion rate.[132]

Mother Teresa did not need to see studies. She was well aware of the connection between contraception and abortion when she said in a speech in the presence of Bill and Hillary Clinton:

> The way to plan the family is Natural Family Planning, not contraception. In destroying the power of giving life, through contraception, a husband or wife is doing something to self. This turns the attention to self and so destroys the gift of love in him or her. In loving, the husband and wife must turn the attention to each other. Once that living love is destroyed by contraception, abortion follows very easily.[133]

68

If couples do not use contraception, won't the world become overpopulated?

Contraceptives are not needed to plan family size. In Calcutta, NFP has proven to be a practical alternative that works effectively. In 1993, the *British Medical Journal* reported, "Indeed, a study of 19,843 poor women in India [practicing NFP to delay pregnancy] had a pregnancy rate approaching zero."[134]

But is there an overpopulation problem? Global fertility and birth rates have been rapidly decreasing for more than twenty-five years.[135] In fact, almost every developed country in the world has a below-replacement fertility rate.[136] At this rate, the global pop-

ulation should top off at seven billion in 2030, and then begin to
sink.[137] Today, humans occupy only one to three percent of the
earth's surface. If you gathered every human being on earth, we
would all fit in Jacksonville, Florida. Everyone could also fit in
Texas, and each person would have more than a thousand square
feet in which to live.[138] This provides more living space than people have in San Francisco, and slightly less than they have in the
Bronx.[139]

The problem is not a lack of space, but an unjust distribution of
resources. "According to the Food and Agriculture Organization,
world food supplies exceed requirements in all world areas."[140]
Besides, farmers use less than half of the land that can be used for
agriculture. Human poverty is the result of bad economic policy,
not overpopulation. (For more on this, see the resource section.)

69

*How reliable are the different kinds of contraception and what are
their side effects?*

There are many methods of contraception, but the most common
are the birth control pill, the condom, Norplant, Depo-Provera,
the diaphragm, spermicides, the intrauterine device (IUD), and
sterilization surgeries. Each method of contraception carries with
it some risk of harmful side effects, many of which are down-
played in our contraceptive culture. Although some are rare, men
and women should be aware of all of the possible consequences.

Sterilization surgeries, such as a tubal ligation or vasectomy do
not have a perfect "success" rate in preventing pregnancies, but
they are very effective (99.6–99.8 percent). However, a woman
who has her tubes tied may experience complications from the
surgery such as severe bleeding or pelvic infection. She will also
be 3.4 times as likely to have a subsequent hysterectomy[141] and
three times as likely to have an ectopic pregnancy (this is when
a baby is conceived but develops outside the uterus; for example,

in the fallopian tubes or the abdominal cavity).[142] She also may experience heavier menstrual bleeding, ovarian tumors, and increased intensity of premenstrual syndrome (PMS) as a result of the decrease in progesterone produced by the ovaries.[143] Besides the physical complications, couples who undergo sterilization often suffer from the guilt and regret of mutilating their bodies. They often experience reduced marital satisfaction.

Men who have vasectomies may be two-and-a-half times as likely to develop kidney stones[144] and they experience an 85 to 90 percent increase in the risk of prostate cancer.[145] Following a vasectomy, a man's testes will still produce sperm. However, because the vas deferens has been severed, the sperm have no way to be released and instead enter the bloodstream, where antibodies have to destroy them. This may lead to diabetes, heart and circulatory diseases, and thyroid and joint disorders.[146] (This does not apply to men who abstain from sex but who have not had a vasectomy, because their sperm are not forced unnaturally into the bloodstream.)

The *birth control pill* has a three-fold mechanism that works to prevent pregnancy. First, the chemicals convince a woman's body that it is constantly pregnant, so that the ovaries do not release eggs, which must be present for fertilization to take place. Sometimes a "breakthrough ovulation" takes place, but the Pill's second mechanism may thicken her cervical mucus, making it difficult for the sperm to travel to the egg.

Should this also fail and the woman becomes pregnant, the Pill has a third mechanism that may cause an early miscarriage, before a woman knows that she is pregnant. While some pills allow ovulation in only about five percent of cycles,[147] research shows that the popular "mini-pill" does not even suppress ovulation for about three of every four women who use it.[148]

Should the woman become pregnant while she is on the Pill, her child's new life is endangered. This is because the Pill chemically alters the lining of the woman's womb (the endometrium), making it hostile to the implantation of an unborn child.[149] In simpler terms, when the child is conceived, the effects of the Pill may keep him from being able to attach in the womb. The child may be aborted without the mother ever knowing it.

Sometimes all three mechanisms fail; for women under twenty-two years of age, the birth control pill has a 4.7 percent failure rate in preventing pregnancy. [150]

For typical sexually active Pill users between the ages of twelve and eighteen, 20 percent of them become pregnant over the course of six months! [151]

There are numerous health risks in taking the Pill, since even the low-dose birth control pills contain steroid hormones that are a thousand times more powerful than any natural hormone in the woman's body. [152] Few young women are informed of the risks. John Wilks, a pharmacist, noted that "It is the only time in medicine when potent drugs are given to a healthy person who then becomes sicker than they were before they started using the drug." [153]

For example, if a woman uses oral contraceptives prior to her first full-term pregnancy, her risk of having breast cancer increases forty percent. [154] Back in the 1970s the studies on this matter went back and forth. But with more time and research, the findings have become more conclusive.

Since 1980, twenty studies have been done on women who have taken oral contraceptives prior to having their first baby. Eighteen of the twenty studies showed that such women have an increased risk of developing breast cancer. [155] This risk increases according to how long she takes the Pill prior to having her first baby. [156] The *Consumer's Guide to the Pill and Other Drugs* states that "Early-age use of the Pill carries a greater risk of breast cancer, of developing larger tumors and having a worse prognosis." [157] Studies also show that "the risk of breast cancer is two to four times higher for women under nineteen years of age who use the Pill compared to women twenty to twenty-four years old because of the rapid tissue and hormonal maturation process in younger women. [158] (See the resource section to study this matter.)

Besides the increased risk of breast cancer, the Pill's potential side effects include moodiness, weight gain, increased blood pressure, gall bladder disease, liver tumors, reduced blood levels of essential vitamins, and the development of depressive personality changes. Several studies indicate an increased risk in contracting HIV. [159] The risk of stroke is five times higher for Pill users as compared to non-Pill users [160] and the risk of heart attack is three times as high. [161]

The Pill also increases a woman's chance of developing cervical cancer, since "the Pill causes the production of a type of cervical mucus which makes it easier for cancer-causing agents to gain access to a woman's body." [162] Beyond this, the Pill increases a woman's chances of infertility [163] and it offers no protection from STDs. If anything, it harms a woman's immune system and decreases her ability to fight off venereal infections. [164] Over one thousand women die each year in the United States from using the birth control pill. [165]

Norplant is another popular form of contraception. It consists of a series of rods or capsules that a doctor inserts into a woman's upper arm. The rods or capsules release progestin that prevents the ovaries from releasing eggs. The implants last for five years, although the effectiveness of Norplant in preventing pregnancy decreases with time. [166] They must be surgically removed.

Norplant works to suppress ovulation in only about fifty percent of cycles, [167] and because it alters the lining of the uterus, it causes first trimester abortions before the mother is aware of her pregnancy. Like the Pill, Norplant provides no protection from STDs. Its potential side effects include: severe lower abdominal pain, prolonged or heavy vaginal bleeding, absence of periods (*amenorrhea*), arm pain and infection, migraine headaches, blurred vision, ovarian cysts (experienced by one in ten users), high blood pressure, increased risk of heart attack or stroke, hair loss, nervousness, liver tumors, and gall bladder disease. [168] Over fifty thousand American women have hired lawyers to assist in their lawsuits against the manufacturer of Norplant, Wyeth-Ayerst. [169]

Depo-Provera is an injection that inhibits ovulation in order to prevent pregnancy for three to six months at a time. It offers no protection from STDs and since breakthrough ovulation occurs about half of the time,[170] it can also cause early abortions, like the Pill and Norplant. Potential side effects of Depo-Provera include: major disturbances of menstrual pattern, prolonged and unpredictable delay in return to fertility, severe and prolonged bleeding, decrease in breast milk production, depression, reduction in libido (sexual desire), a tendency to develop benign and malignant breast lumps, danger to a child in the event of a pregnancy, fetal abnormalities (birth defects)—mainly some masculinizing effects in female children—and a possible link to cervical cancer.[171]

The Medical Institute for Sexual Health also warned, "Recent studies report a decrease in bone density among younger women on Depo-Provera. This may lead to osteoporosis in later stages of life."[172] The two largest studies of women who took Depo-Provera revealed that if a woman took it for between two to three years before the age of twenty-five, she had a 310 percent statistically significant increased risk of getting breast cancer.[173]

The *intrauterine device* is inserted into a woman's uterus, and mainly acts by inducing abortion. The IUD is not as common in America as it used to be, largely because of the lawsuits pending against its manufacturers. Potential side effects include: perforation of the uterus or cervix requiring surgery, increased risk of miscarriage even after it has been removed, tenfold increase in the likelihood of ectopic pregnancies, possible sterility, excessive menstrual bleeding, and increased risk of HIV infection.[174] The effectiveness rate of the IUD in preventing pregnancy is 84 percent.[175]

Spermicides are foams, creams, or gels that are used to kill a man's sperm before it reaches the woman's egg. Studies have shown a link between spermicides and birth defects in children, such as Down Syndrome, limb reduction malformations, and cancerous tissue growths. In regard to its effects on women, there is an increased risk of vaginal infections, and a possible link to increased risk of HIV and other STDs.[176] This mode of contraception fails 30 percent of the time.[177]

The *diaphragm* is a rubber disk that is inserted as a barrier into the woman for the purpose of preventing the sperm from reaching the egg. The diaphragm may cause a local skin irritation because of sensitivity or allergy, and the *New England Journal of Medicine* reported a link between diaphragm use and toxic shock syndrome. This mode of contraception has an 84 percent effectiveness rate, which worsens with the user who is less than thirty years of age.[178]

The male *condom* is a much more common form of contraception, but few people are aware of its disadvantages and failure rate. For example, the condom has not been proven to prevent the transmission of some of the most common STDs. When it comes to preventing HPV (human papillomavirus), some doctors consider the condom to be "useless."[179] Young people often think that the condom has a 99 percent effectiveness rate in preventing pregnancy. However, this figure has been arrived at in laboratories by calculating the size of a man's sperm as compared to the pores in a latex condom. Should a couple use a condom perfectly every time, the failure rate in preventing pregnancy is 2 to 3 percent. But, the condom's typical failure rate in preventing pregnancies among people aged fifteen to twenty-four is 18.4 percent.[180]

It is also becoming clear that barrier methods of contraception, such as the condom and the diaphragm, are potentially harmful to a woman. These methods do not allow the womb's immune system to develop a gradual tolerance to the antigens on sperm and seminal fluid. Imagine that a couple decides to use a barrier method such as the condom for a few years, until they wish to have children. When they try to conceive, the womb is not accustomed to the sperm, and may treat them as foreign bodies. As a result, the woman's immune system may attack the fetus, thereby disrupting the delicate balance of hormones, and causing the woman's blood vessels to constrict, leading to higher blood pressure in the expectant mother.[181]

This condition (preeclampsia) is the third leading cause of maternal death, and it is more than twice as common in women who used barrier methods of contraception.[182]

A man's seminal fluid includes prostaglandins, which are considered among the most potent biological substances known.[183]

During intercourse, the woman's uterus absorbs these and they aid the health of the woman, help mature her uterus,[184] and may protect the mammary gland from cancer.[185]

One researcher described semen as a "built-in prescription formula . . . [that] should be part of the married woman's script for high-level wellness."[186] When a barrier contraceptive obstructs this absorption of the active factors in seminal plasma, the woman is deprived of the beneficial effects of semen. Studies add, "Anything or any method which prevents, retards, or alters the normal degree of physiological absorption of human semen from the vagina carries with it during the early months and years of marriage a risk of future sterility from failure of uterine development and endocrinal asynchronization."[187]

The protective effects of semen are so significant that the *Journal of the American Medical Association* referred to intercourse where barrier contraceptives are used as "unprotected" sexual intercourse,[188] because the woman is not given the natural protection of semen. Another researcher's findings led him to conclude that condom use has "devastating effects" on woman's health.[189]

God has created a woman's body to work in a precise way with a man's. Attempts to thwart that are potentially harmful as well as morally wrong. Pregnancy is not a disease and should not be treated as one.

70

I take the Pill for ovarian cysts and my friend uses it to regulate her cycle, but neither of us is sexually active. Is that a sin?

Although it is wrong to use the birth control pill in order to prevent conception, it has other medical applications. For example, it is often prescribed to treat such conditions as endometriosis, ovarian cysts, irregular cycles, and painful cramps.

It should be noted that some of these conditions have alternative remedies without the adverse side effects of the Pill, including the contraceptive effect. If an alternative therapy exists that avoids these side effects, it should be preferred to the Pill. The Pope Paul VI Institute for the Study of Human Reproduction specializes in such alternatives, so you may wish to contact them using the resource section at the back of this book.

You mention that your friend is using the Pill to "regulate her cycle." She should know that technically the birth control pill does not do this. It may give the appearance of a regular cycle, but it is actually causing her to have a regular "withdrawal bleed" rather than a regular menstruation. If she needs to menstruate regularly, there are other ways of accomplishing this, such as nutritional methods that a doctor can recommend, or the use of progesterone. If your friend is using the Pill for medical reasons, she also should be fully informed of its side-effects, risks, and potential alternatives.

71

What if another pregnancy could put the wife's life at risk? Does the Church say that the couple can not use contraception even for her sake?

If there is a serious danger that another pregnancy could put a woman's life at risk, the couple should avoid pregnancy by means of Natural Family Planning, the most effective method of family planning according to the *British Medical Journal*.[190]

The couple's goal of not endangering the wife's life is good. That is not in question. The issue is the *means* that the couple uses to protect her health. NFP will do that more effectively than most contraceptive methods, and without the side-effects that all forms of contraception carry. It is the better, safer alternative. But even if contraception were more effective than NFP and posed no health risks, it is still intrinsically immoral, and therefore can never be used because it interferes with God's design for how sex is supposed to work.

72

What does the Church teach about in vitro fertilization, artificial insemination, fertility drugs, and stuff like that?

Medical technology exists to promote the proper functioning of our bodies. Men as well as women can be infertile but some of the reproductive methods you are asking about focus on women. Since infertility can be a dysfunction of a woman's reproductive system, the use of fertility drugs which counter this condition and promote the healthy functioning of the reproductive system is morally acceptable. But these must be used responsibly. If they are not, a woman's ovaries may release too many eggs, which may be dangerous to the mother and the child or children.

While reproductive technology may assist the sexual act, it must never replace it. This is partly why the Church does not permit the use of in vitro fertilization (IVF) and artificial insemination. These procedures do not help the marital act, but substitute for it, bringing about conception through a means other than intercourse. In the words of Archbishop Charles Chaput of Denver, "Whether to prevent a pregnancy or achieve one, all techniques which separate the unitive and procreative dimensions of marriage are always wrong." [191] In other words, as contraception tries to make love without making babies, IVF and artificial insemination attempt to make babies without making love. Neither act is moral, because life and love are inseparable. As John Paul II said in an address to President George W. Bush, man must be "the master, not the product, of his technology." [192]

However, there is another, even more serious moral problem with both in vitro fertilization and artificial insemination: Not only do these processes seek to create life in a morally unacceptable way, they also necessarily create *many* "excess" lives that will inevitably be destroyed in their earliest stages. In vitro fertilization (IVF) is a process that involves conceiving life in a laboratory and transferring that into a woman's womb. It is not an easy process, so extra embryos are often frozen and kept for a later attempt or donated or experimented upon. Since many eggs are fertilized during the procedure, a good number of them are destroyed. Commonly, the effort will be a failure and none of the eggs will implant. It is obviously immoral to create and destroy so many lives in an attempt to create one life.

Artificial insemination is a different process, and involves taking the sperm from a man and injecting it into the uterus or placing it in the woman's cervix. This, too, is a difficult method, and it is not uncommon that the process needs to be repeated six or more times in order for it to be successful. Right now, many states do not require STD testing for sperm donors, so HIV and other viruses can be spread during the process. A recent study found that 32 percent of donated sperm contains an STD called human papillomavirus. [193]

Even without these problems, both of these methods are incompatible with the dignity of a child and the life-giving nature of the marital act. Each child should be brought into being by an act of love between his parents, not by a technical researcher tinkering with cells in a petri dish, as in IVF, or a doctor injecting sperm into a uterus, as in artificial insemination. The dignity of human life requires that each person be called into existence within the context of a concrete expression of the covenant between a husband and a wife. When the sperm are taken from a man other than the husband, it also infringes upon the child's right to be born of a father and mother known to him, and it betrays the spouses' marital pledge to become a father and mother only through each other.

Because of contraception and reproductive technologies, we have separated what God has joined together: sex and babies. You may ask, "Well, if these methods are immoral, then why does God let conception occur?" God has entrusted us with the gift of sexuality and he will not prevent us from abusing that freedom. For example, if a child is conceived out of wedlock, the act is immoral, yet God still allows life to come forth from it. Just because conception occurs, that does not mean that the methods to achieve this were good. There are many ways to bring life into the world including marital love, fornication, adultery, rape, incest, IVF, and artificial insemination. Only one, marital love, is consistent with the dignity of the human person and testifies to the truth of God's gift of sexuality.

Many believe that IVF and artificial insemination are the only options available to an infertile couple hoping to have a child of their own. This is not the case. There are many doctors who specialize in determining the cause of infertility and working toward healing that does not replace fertility with technology. See the Pope Paul VI Institute of Human Reproduction in the resource section for more information.

8

Sexually Transmitted Diseases

73

Won't a condom protect you from getting an STD?

This may come as a surprise, but condoms were not invented to prevent STDs. Condoms were made to prevent pregnancy, and only with the epidemic rise in STDs did they get the reputation as a means to enjoy "safe sex." I came across a pamphlet on safe sex at a local university. The final sentence said, "Besides abstinence, condoms provide the best protection against sexually transmitted diseases when used properly!" (I am not sure what the exclamation point was for.)

This pamphlet failed to mention that the National Institutes for Health (NIH) recently published the first thorough review of the scientific research on condom effectiveness. The study examined eight common STDs and found that condoms may reduce the risk of contracting or transmitting only two of them: HIV and gonorrhea (in men). The studies revealed that, even when consistently and correctly used, condoms provide only an 85 percent risk reduction for the transmission of HIV in males and females, and only a 45 to 75 percent risk reduction for the transmission of gonorrhea in males.

While the condom may reduce the likelihood of contracting HIV, yearly cases of this virus are much less than one percent of all the yearly STD cases. [194] Gonorrhea is a much more common problem, but there was not sufficient evidence to conclude that the condom protected women from it. [195] This is not good news for women, because they suffer much greater consequences from being infected by this virus. It can lead to ectopic pregnancy, pelvic inflammatory disease, and infertility.

The report stated that current scientific data fail to provide conclusive evidence that condoms reduce the risk of transmission of
any other STDs. In spite of all the talk today about condoms and
safe sex, they could not prove that condoms offered any protection
to women against seven of the eight STDs reviewed! According
to Dr. John Diggs: "The panel reviewed the medical literature of
the past couple of decades and was unable to prove that condoms
work for herpes, human papillomavirus, trichomonas, chlamydia,
chancroid, or syphilis. The first three alone account for an estimated twelve to twenty million infections per year!"[196]

While the NIH study does not prove that the condom is useless in protecting against the STDs mentioned above, it does mean
that top doctors scouring decades of the best research on condoms
were unable to show their effectiveness.

The study mentioned that there is no evidence that condoms
reduce the risk of human papillomavirus (HPV) infections. I know
of parents who took their infant to the doctor because she had a
sore throat. The doctor examined her and told the parents that the
child had genital warts growing in her throat. Genital warts can
be caused by HPV and usually affect the genital areas of infected
men and women. However, a pregnant woman can transmit them
to her unborn baby and in those cases the virus can cause warts in
the infant's throat. This mother had contracted HPV and passed
it on to her baby in the womb. So much for safe sex.

Further, the failure rate of the condom in preventing pregnancy
is about 14 to 16 percent during the first year of use.[197] Considering that a woman can get pregnant only three to five days out of
the month and STDs can be transmitted every day of the month,
the condom is by no means adequate protection. No matter what
STD we are speaking about, the condom does not guarantee protection even when used consistently and correctly. On the other
hand, chastity guarantees 100 percent protection.

To top it off, one of the only viruses that condom use *has* been
demonstrated to help protect against—HIV—becomes easier to
catch if you happen to have some of the others: The U.S. Department of Health and Human Services has reported that "most

STDs increase the likelihood of transmitting HIV infection at least two- to five-fold." [198]

But the bottom line is this: there is no condom for the heart —or the soul. Whatever we may do to protect our bodies from STDs, if we misuse God's gift of sexuality, there is no protecting our hearts and souls; and if we are faithful with our sexuality, there is no need for protection of any kind, for there is nothing to fear. The very idea of wanting to make sex "safe" is a contradiction in terms. Sex is meant to be a total gift of the self, holding nothing back. Concerns about "safety" should not enter into the equation. You protect yourself from your enemies; you give yourself to your beloved.

74

How do you know if you have an STD?

Some of the symptoms of STDs include blisters, warts, lesions, painful urination, itching, swelling, or unnatural bleeding or discharge. However, many STDs have no obvious symptoms, and *eight out of ten people who have an STD are currently unaware of their infection.* [199] If you have had any genital contact, you should get tested. Many STDs may remain dormant and undetectable for some time, so you could test negative for STDs and still be infected. This is why clinicians recommend that women (and some men) who have been sexually active in the past get tested annually, regardless of their current sexual activity.

Doctors administer different tests to determine the presence of an STD, depending upon the symptoms. If you have ever had intercourse, you should receive all of the following tests: 1. pap smear (for women), and perhaps HPV screening by means of the HPV DNA detection test; 2. Cervical cultures for gonorrhea and chlamydia (for women); 3. Vaginal swabs for trichomonas and bacterial vaginitis (for women); 4. Culture of any ulcers or sores (herpes and syphilis); 5. Blood tests for HIV, hepatitis profile, and syphilis. [200] You may also be tested for other infections by means of a urine sample. People who have engaged in oral or anal sex are at risk of both oral and anal cancers because of some strains of HPV.

When one STD is diagnosed or suspected, there are likely to be more. Since some STDs can lead to sterility in men and women —and even death—you should treat any possible STDs as soon as possible.

75

If I think I have an STD, what should I do? Can I get tested without having to tell my parents?

You should get tested as soon as possible, and since testing can be done on a confidential basis, it is not *necessary* to go with your parents. See the resource section in the back of this book. The number listed under STD Testing will help you to find a good clinic in your area.

Regarding your parents: You may think, "What mom and dad don't know can't hurt them. Besides, if I did tell them, my mom would cry for a week and I would probably be grounded until my forty-seventh birthday." As difficult as this may be, put yourself in your parents' shoes. Imagine you had a child who was sexually active. You would want your child to be able to come to you and be honest about whatever was going on in his or her life.

The sooner you get a real relationship with your folks, the better. Sure, your parents will be upset, but under that hurt are two hearts that want only what is best for you. Perhaps we do not like to tell our parents stuff because of our pride. If we had listened to them in the first place, we would not be in trouble! Swallow the pride, and do what you would want your own child to do. Even if you refuse to tell them, make sure to get tested. Some STDs can be easily cured, but may lead to infertility if they are not treated.

76

I heard that some incurable STD called HPV kills more American women than AIDS. If this is true, what is that, and why are teens not told about it?

What you heard is correct. We hear a lot about HIV and some other STDs, but we never seem to hear about human papillomavirus—even though it is the number one reason why women visit the gynecologist.[201] HPV causes 99.7 percent of cervical cancer, and in the United States this kills more women each year than AIDS.[202] Worldwide, it takes the lives of five hundred thousand women annually.[203]

Not all people who contract HPV will develop cervical cancer, and only one percent of all individuals who have been infected with HPV have genital warts.[204] Therefore, even if a person is free of warts, he or she might still have HPV. There are over one hundred different types of HPV[205] and most of those that cause genital warts are not associated with cancer,[206] but one person can have multiple types at once. Because the virus is widespread and can remain latent for a considerable time, clinicians recommend a yearly pap smear for any woman who has been sexually active, even if she is now abstinent. HPV DNA tests are now available as well, but these can only be used on women.

To give you an idea of how large the problem is, according to the Medical Institute for Sexual Health, "Approximately 75 percent of sexually active individuals are now, or have previously been, infected with HPV."[207] The National Institutes of Health reported that, "HPV infection of the genital tract can be detected in approximately 30 percent of sexually active adolescent girls and young women."[208]

One reason it has spread so quickly is that people are unaware the virus can be contracted through any genital contact (genital, oral, or by means of the hands). It should also be said that many people who contract HPV will not be harmed by it. Although it is incurable, this does not mean that it is permanent, like herpes.

Many strains of HPV are not considered to be "high risk," and the body usually fights HPV off on its own. Other times, the virus may remain latent for decades. A teenage girl may contract HPV and not suffer health effects from the infection until her thirties or forties.

Why don't we hear much about it? There are two reasons. First, the full effects of the epidemic will not be known for over a decade. HPV sometimes manifests itself through warts, but more often the infection is sub-clinical and invisible to the naked eye. Most teens who have HPV show no symptoms, and so they do not bother to get checked for it. Even when they do get checked, the doctor's colposcope may miss 20 to 70 percent of genital wart infestations.[209]

The second reason we do not hear much about HPV is that it is the Achilles' heel of the "safe sex" campaign. According to the Centers for Disease Control (CDC), "Studies which have attempted to assess male condom benefit for women have generally found no evidence of protection against infection."[210] According to the American Cancer Society, "Condoms cannot protect against infection with HPV."[211]

77

How many STDs are out there, and can you describe some of the really common ones?

In the 1960s, gonorrhea and syphilis were the only major STDs, and both of these could be treated with penicillin. Today, there are over fifty different STDs, and some of the most common ones are without cures.[212] Furthermore, the majority of people who have an STD are unaware of their own contagious state.[213]

The four STDs that are incurable are HPV, HIV, herpes, and hepatitis. All of the others have various forms of successful treatments. Some of the most common STDs include HPV, chlamydia, herpes, gonorrhea, and trichomonas. I discussed HPV above. Let's take a look at some of the others.

Chlamydia is the most common bacterial STD, and is found primarily among teenage girls and young women.[214] It is estimated that forty percent of sexually active single women have been infected at some time with chlamydia.[215] The disease is so common that there are more cases of chlamydia reported than all cases of AIDS, chancroid, gonorrhea, hepatitis (types A, B, and C), and syphilis *combined.*[216] Condoms have not been demonstrated to eliminate the risk of chlamydia.[217]

Some of the symptoms include vaginal or urethral discharge, burning with urination, pelvic pain, and genital ulcers. Men can experience many of these and also tenderness of the scrotum. The presence of the disease probably also increases a person's risk of contracting HIV.[218] In women, chlamydia may spread to the uterus and fallopian tubes, causing pelvic inflammatory disease (PID) This can lead to infertility, and may become a life threatening infection. One out of three women who are infertile are so because of PID.[219]

Unfortunately, as many as 85 percent of women (and 40 percent of men) who are infected with chlamydia show no symptoms.[220] Since the victims are often asymptomatic, they do not receive treatment with the necessary oral antibiotics. For this reason, chlamydia is called the "silent sterilizer." A female who acquires chlamydia from an infected partner runs the risk of never being able to have children. Since one in five newly married American couples is infertile, this epidemic is never far from us.[221] Think, girls: is this guy worth your uterus?

If a woman's fertility is not lost, PID can still cause scarring in the fallopian tubes, which increases her risk of having an ectopic (tubal) pregnancy. PID is also the leading cause of maternal death in the first trimester of pregnancy.[222] Should a woman contract chlamydia and still conceive successfully, it is possible for her to pass the infection on to her baby during childbirth. This can cause blindness in the baby.[223]

Herpes is a virus that infects the skin and mucous membranes such as the mouth and genitals. Thirty to 40 percent of sexually active single Americans are infected with herpes, which is incurable and highly contagious.[224] Herpes type one primarily causes oral infections but can be transmitted to the genitals via oral sex. Type two can be transferred to the mouth from the genitals. In other words, these can be transmitted without intercourse. Unlike many other STDs that are spread by means of bodily fluid, herpes is spread by skin-to-skin contact. Not only a person's genitals, but his or her abdomen, thighs, hands, and other areas can be infected. Herpes can be picked up through contact with these areas and transmitted without symptoms. Because of this, the condom can only provide partial protection at best.

Within a week of contracting herpes, a person may have preliminary symptoms including fever, headache, and muscle aches. Lesions then appear where the virus was contracted. The lesions usually begin as small blisters before breaking and becoming ulcers. Other symptoms include itching, burning with urination, vaginal discharge, and swollen lymph nodes in the groin area. Since herpes is incurable, it is not uncommon for infected people to have recurrent outbreaks of lesions for the rest of their lives.

It has been estimated that 90 percent of people infected with genital herpes are unaware that they are infected.[225] This is especially worrisome since people with herpes are at an increased risk of contracting HIV. Symptom-free but infected individuals may pass the herpes virus on unknowingly.[226] It is not uncommon for an infected mother to pass the disease on to her newborn child, and when this occurs the child may die.[227] The American College of Obstetricians and Gynecologists said, "The use of a condom doesn't provide reliable protection against herpes."[228] Do not expect a condom to protect your future spouse and children from the effects of this STD.

Gonorrhea is one of the most common bacterial STDs in America. It is highly contagious, and can be transmitted by means of intercourse, oral sex, and anal sex. Infected mothers may also pass the disease to their babies during birth. Symptoms vary depending upon what part of the body is infected. Some experience a discharge from the genitals and painful urination. Women can suffer from abnormal bleeding and men from swelling around the testicles. In a woman, the infection may spread to her uterus and fallopian tubes, leading to pelvic inflammatory disease, which, as we have seen, can cause infertility. Up to 50 percent of males and 80 percent of females who are infected have no symptoms.[229] The disease can remain undetected even though the person's mouth may be infected. Condom use does not eliminate the risk of contracting gonorrhea; if the disease is contracted, it must be treated with antibiotics.[230]

Trichomonas is a protozoan that infects the genital tract. It is estimated that up to ten percent of American woman have it, but the majority do not know that they are infected. Trichomonas often leads to vaginitis, cervicitis, abnormal bleeding, swelling, itching, abdominal pain, and other symptoms. The person may also become more susceptible to contracting HIV. There is insufficient evidence to determine whether the condom can offer protection from this disease, but it can be treated with medication.[231]

When considering the potential impact of STDs, we should remember the words of former U.S. Surgeon General C. Everett Koop: "When you have sex with someone, you are having sex with everyone they have had sex with for the last ten years, and everyone they and their partners have had sex with for the last ten years."[232] Further, people can get tested for STDs, be told that they are clean, and then transmit all sorts of dormant STDs the tests did not detect. Most tests today pick up over 90 percent of the infections they are testing for. The problem is that many people believe they have been tested for all STDs when, in reality, they have only been tested for a few.

Recently, a high school girl contacted me because she was considering sleeping with her boyfriend. She was a virgin, but he had been with eleven girls. If you do the math, you will see that if his previous partners were as sexually active as he had been (and, depending on the types of STDs), she could be exposing herself to the possible infections of more than two thousand people if she slept with him once.[233] Wisely, she chose not to take the risk.

78

I have heard that teenage girls are at a high risk of getting STDs. Why is that?

Women are more susceptible to STDs than men because of the nature of their reproductive organs. Many STDs survive best where it is dark, moist, and warm. Female genitalia is interior, and male genitalia is exterior, so the woman's body is more easily infected. Because the woman's infections are often hidden on the inside, they are not easy to see.

The risk of infection is greater for young women. The cervix of a teenager is immature and covered with a tissue known as the ectropion. The ectropion has a large surface area that is more susceptible to infection than that of an older woman's due to its size. When a woman reaches her mid-twenties, the ectropion will have matured, decreased in size, and been replaced by a tissue that is more resistant to infections from STDs.[234] For example, a fifteen-year-old girl who is sexually active is ten times as likely as a sexually active twenty-four-year-old to develop pelvic inflammatory disease (PID), the most rapidly increasing cause of infertility in the United States.[235]

The birth control pill also increases a young woman's chance of contracting an STD because it suppresses her immune system.[236] According to the Medical Institute of Sexual Health, "The hormones in birth control pills may cause changes in the cervix that make chlamydial infection more likely to occur."[237] The Pill also causes the production of a certain type of cervical mucous that makes it easier for cancer-causing agents to have access to a woman's body.[238] According to the *Consumer's Guide to the Pill and Other Drugs*, "The link between the Pill and cervical cancer has been established by medical researchers and is proven beyond doubt."[239]

It has also been discovered that the woman's body is "designed to come to recognize and accept one man's sperm and to reject other sperm,"[240] and that if a woman has three or more sexual partners in a lifetime, she is fifteen times as likely to get cervical cancer.

As science proves, a woman's body is like her heart—it is not designed for multiple sexual partners.

9

Purity Renewed

79

Can God forgive you if you have had premarital sex?

Yes. The Bible says, "To the penitent he provides a way back, he encourages those who are losing hope! . . . Turn again to the Most High and away from sin" (Sir. 17:19, 21, NAB). If we repent he will forgive any sin, including premarital sex. In the Gospel of John, a crowd wanted to kill a woman who was caught in sexual sin. Jesus sent the people away to think about their own sins. When they left, he asked, " 'Woman, where are they? Has no one condemned you?' She said, 'No one, Lord.' And Jesus said, 'Neither do I condemn you; go, and do not sin again' " (John 8:1-11).

Over and over, Scripture says the exact same thing. Psalm 103:12 reads, "As far as the east is from the west, so far does he remove our transgressions from us." Lamentations 3:22-23 states, "His mercies never come to an end; they are new every morning." God holds no grudges and does not look down on us because of the past. On the contrary, he says, "I have swept away your transgressions like a cloud, and your sins like mist; return to me, for I have redeemed you. . . . I will not remember your sins" (Is. 44:22, 43:25).

The history of the Church tells the same story. Many saints and heroes of the faith led immoral lives or committed grave sins before repenting and leading lives of exemplary holiness, including King David, Mary Magdalene, Paul, and Augustine. The sins these saints repented of include premarital sex, adultery, and even murder. Just as God forgave them, he can and will forgive us, if we are willing to do what they did—repent and amend our ways.

Come to him in prayer. He will not be thinking, "Oh, here comes that kid who did all that stuff at that party." Instead, he is thinking the same thing he was thinking thousands of years ago: "Fear not, for I have redeemed you; I have called you by name, you are mine. . . . Behold, I have graven you on the palms of my hands" (Is. 43:1; 49:16). The greatest sin you have ever committed is like a grain of sand next to the mountain of his mercies.

Jesus instituted the sacrament of reconciliation to bring the gift of his forgiveness to us. After he rose from the dead, he came to the apostles, greeted them, and then breathed on them. The only other place in the Bible where God breathes on anyone is at the moment of creation. So we know something big is happening here. Jesus then said, "If you forgive the sins of any, they are forgiven; if you retain the sins of any, they are retained" (John 20:21–23).

For two thousand years, the Church has made this healing gift from Jesus available to us, so that we can hear the consoling words of absolution: "God, the Father of mercies, through the death and resurrection of his Son has reconciled the world to himself and sent the Holy Spirit among us for the forgiveness of sins; through the ministry of the Church may God give you pardon and peace, and I absolve you from your sins in the name of the Father, and of the Son, and of the Holy Spirit."

Come to the great sacrament of reconciliation, and receive the gift of God's forgiveness.

80

I have been with a lot of guys in high school, and I have a horrible reputation. I am going to college in the fall, and I am looking forward to starting with a clean slate. Is it possible to become innocent again?

I had a friend in college who looked up to a young woman I will call "Rachel." Rachel was a resident assistant (RA) in my friend's dormitory and she was a campus leader. More importantly, Rachel seemed to reflect the love of Jesus to everyone who crossed her path. My friend always admired how pure and innocent she was. One night, this RA shared her testimony with my friend. Rachel had been sexually active throughout high school, but chose to accept God's invitation and turn her life around. My friend was astonished as Rachel opened her heart and revealed how Christ had made her a new creation. She has since married a great man of God and they have begun to raise a beautiful family.

This young woman was living proof of Paul's words: "Therefore, if any one is in Christ, he is a new creation; the old has passed away, behold, the new has come. All this is from God, who through Christ reconciled us to himself" (2 Cor. 5:17-18). Notice that Paul says that this is from God, not from us. The only thing we really own is our sin. All we can do is come to the Lord in our woundedness and allow him to work his miracles.

Do not let yourself fall into despair, thinking, "I already gave my virginity away, so what does it matter now? Once it's gone it's gone. What use am I to God, and what good guy would want me now?" One young woman said that after she lost her virginity, "I've never hated myself more. But it was done. My virginity was gone. Never could I get it back. It didn't matter after that, so sex became an everyday occurrence. My only fear was losing Bobby —he was the first—and even if he treated me badly (and there were those times), I was going to do anything I could to hang on to him."[241] Christ is there for you now, and he calls you to cling to him. He still has a plan for your life.

Remember when Jesus fed the multitudes in the Gospel of Matthew? He asked how much food they had and they brought him five loaves and two fish—not much if you need to feed five thousand, not counting women and children. He took what little they had, multiplied it, fed the thousands, and had enough left over to fill twelve baskets (Matt. 14:13-21). We can learn from this that it does not matter how little we have to give him. What matters is how fully we give what little we have. He will take care of the miracle in you. You just come to him to be loved by him as you are. Jesus will take our sins of scarlet, and in their place paint an image of his mercy for the world to see. In the words of the prophet Isaiah, "Though your sins are like scarlet, they shall be as white as snow; though they are red like crimson, they shall become like wool" (Is. 1:18).

The question is not whether Christ can make you a new creation, but whether you have faith that he will. He says to you as he said to the blind men in the Gospel of Matthew: "Do you believe that I am able to do this?" (Matt. 9:28). Say yes, and pray as David did in the Psalms, "Create in me a clean heart, O God, and put a new and right spirit within me" (Ps. 51:10). And remember that Jesus said, "Whatever you ask in my name, I will do it" (John 14:13). God will give you this clean slate, a purity that you can guard and build on.

81

I have made some big mistakes in the past, but I do not know how to bring this up with the guy I am seeing right now, or even if I should. What would you recommend?

Do not feel that you should tell a guy all about your past just because you are in a relationship with him. If the relationship is serious and possibly heading toward marriage, then it is good to be honest with him regarding these issues. However, pray about the timing of this and do not feel pressured to pour everything out. Be general, and admit that you made some mistakes in past relationships, and you really want this relationship to be pure and focused on God. As time progresses and you feel comfortable and the timing seems right, you may want to disclose more.

If and when this happens, keep the following in mind: Do not be overly explicit in explaining everything that happened. These details could harm the guy you are seeing. Without being in any way dishonest, be prudent about how much you disclose. You might not end up marrying this man but if you have shared every single memory and hurt, then the emotional bond you have created could make it difficult to break things off. Also, it would be troubling to know that this man who is not your husband knows things about you that only your husband should know.

If you do end up marrying him, reassure him of how much he means to you. A study of 130 couples with strong marriages found that most of the husbands reported that their wives knew how to make them feel good about themselves.[242] Do not talk a lot about how intimate you have been with other men. Simply reaffirm in his heart that he is your man. Frequently, the previous intimacies of one spouse will cause feelings of pain, inferiority, or resentment in the other partner. So love him all the more to quell any discomfort he may have about feeling compared to others.

Finally, since you may not have the gift of your virginity left to give him, here is a suggestion. A friend of mine lost her virginity during high school, and had multiple sexual partners. Instead of giving in to despair that she would have nothing left to give her future husband, she came up with a beautiful idea. She went to prayer, made a commitment to reclaim her purity, and wrote a letter of encouragement to herself to stay firm in this resolve. She listed all the reasons she would no longer lead a sexually promiscuous life. My friend included in this letter all the things she hoped for in a future husband and promised to wait for God to bring them together. Now when she feels tempted to return to her former life, she pulls this letter out and reminds herself that true love is possible, and that she should save herself for her future husband. Each time she reads the letter, she adds to it, and writes to her future husband.

This letter is a constant support for her, and each time she adds to it she becomes stronger in her convictions. She now has a large envelope filled with many pages that she is waiting to give to her husband on their wedding day. What a comfort and a blessing this will be to him—to see that although she made mistakes, she turned her life around and saved herself for him. She could have said: "It's too late for me. Once your virginity is gone it's gone. I might as well forget about ever being pure again." Instead, she trusted in the Lord and had faith that he is never outdone in generosity. It is never too late. Have courage and trust in God for a godly husband. You are worth it.

82

I am dating someone with a sinful past who has made an incredible conversion and is really pure now. The problem is that what this person did keeps haunting me. Any suggestions on how to get beyond this?

One reason why these thoughts keep coming to mind is because you are probably trying to push them down and out of your mind without dealing with them. Sweeping them under the rug will just allow them to keep coming back to bug you. As I see it, the solution is not to repress these thoughts but to deal with them by accepting them and lifting them up. Whenever you have these troubling thoughts, do two things.

First, offer that pain in your heart for the person's healing, for your date's former partners, and for all those that are living in sin. Do not dwell on the past, but offer those thoughts to Jesus and his Mother when they come to mind. Give thanks that the Lord has brought your date away from that lifestyle, and pray for the souls that are still held by sin. Our sufferings have redemptive value because of Christ's sufferings, so know that Jesus can use your suffering. You need to realize the good that the Lord can do through it.

Secondly, resolve never to lead your date into sin. The Lord will heal you both as he knows best. In the meantime, let the pain become a prayer.

83

A guy I barely knew raped me at a party. What should I do, and how do I heal from this emotionally?

I am so sorry to hear what you have been through. I have several friends who have been through the same thing, and there are a number of things you can do.

First of all, a man who forces himself on a woman has committed a crime as well as a sin. If you have been raped, you should discuss it with your parents. Among the things you need to talk about are the possibilities of getting counseling and pressing charges; after all, the guy may do the same thing to someone else.

Emotional and spiritual healing involves several different things. You will need to learn to let go of the pain, and not let hatred and bitterness take root in your heart. When painful memories come back to you, learn to transform that pain into prayer. Since Jesus said to pray even for our enemies, pray for the man who hurt you. The more anger or hatred you feel toward him, the more you will need to conquer that anger and hatred—for your sake as well as his. Pray that he may encounter Christ and that he may realize what it means to be a man. By praying for him as Jesus prayed for those who put him to death, you will be practicing the essence of forgiveness, namely, continuing to will the other person's good. Forgiveness does not mean that you ignore what he did to you or that you do not press charges. It means that you allow Christ's love rather than your own pain and anger to determine your attitude toward this man. He is a sinner Christ died for.

Increase your prayer time as well, since God is a healer of wounds seen and unseen. As the healing process begins, do not think that no guy will ever love you. This man took from you but you still have yourself to give. Remember: You did not give yourself to him. Also, know that being raped is not a sin. Where there is no consent, there is no sin.

Finally, take a look at your social group and see if this is really the best bunch for you. Check out church youth groups in your area. Faithful, solid friends are priceless. In the words of Sirach, "A faithful friend is a sturdy shelter: he that has found one has found a treasure" (6:14). I also recommend that you visit with a priest or counselor. You are not alone in this, and they are there to give you the help that I cannot.

84

What can I do in the future to prevent being raped?

Here are a few practical tips for how to avoid being a victim of rape. Do not allow yourself to become isolated with a guy you do not know or trust. If you are at a party, stick close to your friends, and look out for each other. Drugs and alcohol are factors that make rape and sexual mistakes much more common, so stay clear of these. If you are of age to drink, know your limit and do not leave your drink unattended. If you are on a date with a guy, be straightforward about your boundaries. Of course, a gentleman should always respect your "No" or "Stop" no matter what, but too much intimacy creates sexual momentum, and even a guy who intends to respect your wishes might not always stop when you want him to. Out of respect for him as well as for yourself, save sexual arousal for marriage.

85

Is it okay for a girl to have an abortion if she was raped?

A few years ago in the former Yugoslavia, a group of soldiers broke into a convent and raped a nun named Sister Lucy Vertrusc. As a result of the rape, she became pregnant. Sister Lucy was faced with a decision: Do I keep this child, whose face will be an icon of the man who raped me? She chose life, and said, "I will be a mother. The child will be mine and no one else's. . . . Someone has to begin to break the chain of hatred that has always destroyed our countries. And so, I will teach my child only one thing: love. This child, born of violence, will be a witness along with me that the only greatness that gives honor to a human being is forgiveness."[243] She knew that the baby did not deserve the death penalty for the crime his father committed.

Women who abort children who were conceived by rape often say that it took longer to recover from the abortion than from the rape. When a woman has been raped, has she not suffered enough emotional pain? Will she be comforted when the suffering of the rape is compounded with the guilt of knowing that she took her child's life? Has she not been violated enough? Now is the time when she needs to be supported by and immersed in love, so that some good can come from the tragedy of the rape.

Not only does abortion cause profound emotional damage to a woman, researchers have found that having an abortion lowers a woman's life expectancy. Her body cannot handle the trauma of terminating a pregnancy in such an unnatural and violent manner. Research shows that if a girl under the age of eighteen has an abortion when the child is more than eight weeks old, the mother's chance of having breast cancer rises 800 percent.[244]

Other risks of abortion include laceration of the cervix, perforated uterus, pulmonary embolism, shock, the need for a hysterectomy, swelling of the brain, coma, convulsions, kidney failure, pelvic inflammatory disease, sterility, a 50 percent increase in spontaneous miscarriage, a 200 percent increase in ectopic pregnancy, and maternal death.[245] This is no way to treat a woman who has suffered enough because of rape.

If you know of a woman who is pregnant and unmarried, see the resources in the back of the book for ways you can help her.

86

I want to start over, but I can't give up sex. What should I do to get back on track?

I recommend six steps to get back on track:

1. *Recognize* your mistakes and admit your faults, but do not let yourself get preoccupied with them. Like everyone else, you are not perfect, so give yourself the freedom to forgive yourself and then decide to overcome your weakness. You have to want healing for yourself.

Recognizing your faults is one side of the coin, but recognizing that you deserve respect is the other. Many people who have fallen into sexual sins have lost all self-respect. They feel that there is no point in turning back, but even if they wanted to turn back it would be impossible, and that even if it were possible, no one would love them after all they have done. You do deserve respect, but you have to respect yourself first. When we commit sexual sin, we lose respect for our bodies and for the bodies of others. When this happens, it becomes easier and easier to fall into unhealthy physical relationships. Only you can choose to break out of this. It is important that you know from the get-go that the healing process will demand work and sacrifice on your part.

2. *Repent.* You have realized that you do have a problem, so come to God as his child, asking for his grace. Ask him to forgive you and heal you, not only of this area of weakness, but also of any other wounds or vulnerabilities, however deep or old they might be, that might have contributed to your problem in this area. As Jesus said, "Apart from me you can do nothing" (John 15:5). You are wholly dependent upon God to get out of this and he is wholly capable of finishing the good work that he has begun in you. The Holy Spirit is already alive in you, moving you to recognize your problem and seek a new beginning. God is at work in you; he has not abandoned you.

Come to him in the great sacrament of reconciliation and experience his mercies. He forgives, heals, restores, and encourages us, but we must come to him with sincere hearts: "A broken and contrite heart, O God, thou wilt not despise" (Ps. 51:17).

3. *Resist* the temptation to give in to destructive thinking: "I'm a bad person, I don't deserve real love, and I need sex. I'm addicted —I can't help myself." None of those things is true! People tell themselves that they are addicted to things like sex in order to make themselves feel like they do not have any control over their behavior so that they can keep indulging in it. But it is not *true*. You do have control, and you do have dignity. You are a son or daughter of God. That is your identity—your identity is not as a "bad person." Sure, you have made mistakes. But do not identify yourself by them.

You *are* worthy of love, because that is what God has created you for. When you make mistakes, you do not forfeit your worthiness to receive love. Also, you do not "need" sex. Perhaps you have formed an attachment to the pleasure of sex or to its emotional intimacy. Perhaps sex has become for you a way to avoid genuine relationships. Instead of using sex to express intimacy, you may be using it to escape intimacy. God's grace is stronger than those chains and he will give you a greater love if you cling to him. Your desires will not disappear when you come to him, but he will give you his love so that you will be able to overcome the temptations.

4. *Refrain* from bad relationships, and make a clean break from any unhealthy relationships that you are in now. These drive you deeper into loneliness. Sometimes breaking them off is easy. The hard part is not running back to them. This is when you must run to God instead.

When we use sex to feel secure, we end up feeling more insecure than ever, and we may be tempted to jump into sexual acts to deal with our fear of not being lovable. It becomes a vicious cycle. It is then that you must come back to God with all your heart. Do not let fear stand in the way and do not run elsewhere to find the fulfillment and wholeness that only he can give.

5. *Resolve* to live in purity. Part of the process is moving away from bad situations, but the other half is moving into good ones. Make that decision that no one else can make for you. You have to want it for yourself, so set your guidelines, write them down before you enter a relationship, and stick by them.

Josh McDowell said, "After interviewing thousands of young people, I am convinced that many teens and young singles are sexually active not because they really want to be, but because they don't have any deep personal reasons for waiting until they are married."[246]

You need a vision of real love, a hope that will make it easier for you to forego the passing traps of lust in favor of a better and more beautiful kind of life and love. It does exist. So go for purity and make a conscious effort to do things differently in the future.

Change the way you approach relationships. It is a sign of maturity to seek the advice of older and wiser people, particularly our parents. Parents are not always available, so go to a good priest, youth minister, relative, or other mentor to get input on your relationships.

Also, look at your selection of friends, music, magazines, movies, and other things that influence you. See if you can get involved in a local youth group, Bible study, or prayer group at school or church. This may be stepping out of your usual social circles, but you need that support and fellowship. As a reminder to yourself and a sign to others of your commitment, you could wear a ring to symbolize your commitment to chastity.

Also, check out the resources in the back of this book for good reading and web sites. It is good to read on your own but it is far better to find a good priest or counselor with whom you can speak openly and regularly about your struggles. A wise counselor will be able to discern the extent of your problem and lead you on the path to purity.

6. *Renew* yourself through prayer. It is essential to know that you are deeply loved by God, so set a prayer time for each day. He will work wonders in you, and he has so much that he is waiting to tell you and so much that he wants to give you. The best is yet

to come (Jer. 29:11–14). If you are serious about wanting true love, a new path awaits, but only you can make that decision to be generous with God.

87

I have gone to confession, but I can't forgive myself for what I did. How do you get over the feelings of guilt and regret, and forget the bad experiences?

As you are realizing, sin often leaves deep wounds in the heart. During this difficult time when you may want nothing more than to move on and feel forgiven, keep the following points in mind.

Consider the story of the prodigal son. He returned home to his father and said, "I have sinned against heaven and before you; I am no longer worthy to be called your son" (Luke 15:21). Look at the father's reaction. He ran to meet his son, threw the finest robes on him, put rings on his fingers, welcomed him with open arms, and threw a party. The son stopped moping and accepted the father's merciful love. He did not sit outside the celebration, but allowed his father to rejoice that he had returned. The father's joy embraced the son. This parable not only tells us of God's mercy, it also shows us how to accept his forgiveness. We might feel as if our sins make us unworthy to be a child of God, but when we repent the Father looks into our eyes and sees his own life within us. He sees his own Son within us.

Nevertheless, it is true that sexual wounds take time to heal. Be patient and do not beat yourself up. All of us must come to terms with the parts of our past we wish we could erase. We are all sinners, and God's work of restoring us to wholeness is one that will unfold in time. As he works to heal you, these feelings of remorse are bound to come to the surface.

In some ways, forgiving yourself for your own mistakes is similar to forgiving someone else who has hurt you. Forgiveness does not necessarily mean that you do not feel the pain any more. In the words of the *Catechism of the Catholic Church*: "It is not in our power not to feel or to forget an offense; but the heart that offers itself to the Holy Spirit turns injury into compassion and purifies the memory in transforming the hurt into intercession."[247]

The pain you feel over your own failures can be transformed in the same way. The bad memories and wounds of sin that rush back into your mind can actually be used as a way to heal the past. Because the past sometimes hurts, we try to suppress the memories and shove them to a place in our mind where they will stop haunting us. There is a better way. When the hurts of the past weigh upon your heart, take those pains and offer them as a prayer for all who may have been hurt in these past experiences —including yourself. When the flashbacks happen, take that as a reminder to offer up a prayer for healing.

In time, God will heal the past, and you may think about it less often. Let him work on that. Your task is to ask his forgiveness and to draw close to him. Do not give in to despair, thinking that you are no use to God because you made some mistakes. Look at Rahab in the Old Testament. She was a prostitute who turned back to God, and Jesus was a descendant of hers.

Also, realize that God wants to purify you not only for your sake, but for the sake of those you will lead to him. The Lord will be able to use you and your past to reach and heal others who are going through the same difficulties that you have been through. You are in a position to reach hearts that no one else could reach. Listen to God's voice if he calls you to help others in big or small ways in the apostolate of purity. By ministering to others in this way, you will regain a sense of wholeness and peace. You will see for yourself that God can write straight with crooked lines. As God said through the prophet Jeremiah, "If you repent so that I restore you, in my presence you shall stand. . . . You shall be my mouthpiece" (Jer. 15:19, NAB).

It is also good to recognize that *living purely in future relationships will begin to heal the past.* Relationships can actually be healing, not scarring. To get relationships off in the right direction, be up front with regard to your values, and do not wait for an intimate moment to decide or announce your guidelines.

Finally, remember that forgiveness is not a feeling. Sometimes feelings of consolation are present, but when they are not, we need to trust that God has still forgiven us. His mercy is a free gift from a good God. Hannah Arendt wrote: "Without being forgiven, released from the consequences of what we have done, our capacity to act would, as it were, be confined to a single deed from which we could never recover; we would remain the victims of its consequences forever."[248] Thankfully, because of the death and resurrection of Christ, the debt of our sins has been paid, and we are free to call God our *Abba*, Father.

Realize that your worth rests in God and that he loves you.

88

I have been through a lot of really bad relationships. How can I learn to trust a guy again?

Begin by jumping headlong into an intense, intimate relationship with a trustworthy guy—Jesus. The more you get to know him, the more you will be able to recognize guys that resemble him, and guys that do not. Recognize that the ones who are most like him are most worthy of trust, but do not be quick to give your heart away. The Lord can heal anything, but the healing of wounds and the rebuilding of trust is a process that takes time.

Also, do not think that you always need to be in a relationship —especially in high school. Take some time for just you and God. Having alone time with the Lord is a part of the healing process. In addition, having God-centered relationships will help to mend the wounds of the past. To find the healing and love that you truly deserve, turn to God and follow his lead in your relationships.

In the future, keep the following considerations in mind when choosing your companions. Do not date someone if you can not see yourself marrying him. Do not marry someone unless he loves God more than he loves you. Do not carry on a relationship with a guy who is unable to resist temptation. If he is unable to refuse temptation before marriage, how will he refuse temptation after marriage? What woman wants to marry a guy who can not say no to sex?

89

What if I feel like I don't deserve a good guy? Will someone still love me even if I made some mistakes and am carrying "baggage"?

You may think that the holier a guy is, the less likely he would be to accept you with your "baggage." Actually, the opposite is true. The Bible speaks repeatedly of God as the bridegroom and his people as the bride. When Israel turned away from God in the Old Testament, it was described as an act of spiritual adultery. In the book of Hosea, it is written, "the land commits great harlotry by forsaking the Lord. . . . She . . . decked herself with her ring and jewelry, and went after her lovers, and forgot me, says the Lord" (Hos. 1:2, 2:13). Even so, the Lord took her in: "I will betroth you to me for ever; I will betroth you to me in righteousness and in justice, in steadfast love, and in mercy. I will betroth you to me in faithfulness; and you shall know the Lord. . . ." "But they did not know that I healed them" (Hos. 2:19–20; 11:3).

When a "good guy" loves and accepts a girl who has a checkered past, it is an act of love in imitation of the heavenly Father. God loved Israel even when she was impure, and a "good guy" is able to love a woman even if she has an impure past. Through the work of redemption God purifies his bride, "that he might present the church to himself in splendor, without spot or wrinkle or any such thing, that she might be holy and without blemish" (Eph. 5:27). Similarly, by living purely with you, a godly man can help you heal your memories. The more a man is like God, the more he will be able to love you as God loves us, with all of your baggage. He loves us where we are, but loves us too much to leave us there.

None of us deserves the gifts that God bestows upon us. His generosity is unimaginable. "From of old no one has heard or perceived by the ear, no eye has seen a God besides thee, who works for those who wait for him" (Is. 64:4). "Shall I not open for you the floodgates of heaven, to pour down blessing upon you without measure?" (Mal. 3:10, NAB).

The truth is, we have all made mistakes. Even good guys have plenty of baggage. Suppose, though, that you met a young man who had a checkered past. Would you refuse to accept him? If you would accept such a man, then why would a good guy refuse to accept you? Keep hope alive, and may the following words from a husband to his wife (who had slept with another man before marriage) be a comfort for you: "I was always held to a higher standard by you than by any other girl I ever dated. You were strong, uncompromised, and pure. That's all I know of you. That's all that matters to me."[249] Do not be afraid that you will not find a good guy or that you will not have a successful marriage. The absence of physical virginity does not doom marriages, but the absence of the virtue of chastity does.

How to Stay Pure

90

What can my girlfriend and I do on dates so that we do not end up going too far?

Step number one begins before a date: If you are serious about the virtue of chastity, then pray often for the grace to be pure and to avoid temptations. As Mother Teresa said, "To be pure, to remain pure, can only come at a price, the price of knowing God and loving him enough to do his will. He will always give us the strength we need to keep purity as something beautiful for God. Purity is the fruit of prayer."[250]

"How can a young man keep his way pure?" Scripture asks. "By guarding it according to thy word. With my whole heart I seek thee; let me not wander from thy commandments! I have laid up thy word in my heart, that I might not sin against thee" (Ps. 119:9–11). Stay near to Christ, since he is the source of purity. A couple who draws near to Jesus allows his love to flow through them to each other. They get out of the way, and let him provide the love that exists between them. This is purity of heart, a life of intimacy with God.

Prayer is our first priority. After that, we need to set guidelines in order to avoid temptations. If you are sitting on a couch kissing a girl, it is not the best time to start thinking about your boundaries. Know them in advance, because your judgment will be anything but objective during an intense situation.

What should you do during a date? Here is a great way to get going in the right direction (a friend of mine at San Diego State University actually went on a date just like this and recommended it to me). Pick up your girlfriend and head off to church on a

Saturday afternoon. Go to reconciliation, and then take some time to talk about your relationship. Prayerfully set some firm boundaries regarding intimate behavior. Talking about these things will open up communication and contribute to a healthy relationship. Often, couples who establish these boundaries and goals describe feeling a new sense of freedom, peace, and security in the relationship.

While discussing your boundaries, you may realize that the two of you are wired differently. For example, a woman needs to realize that a man's body works differently than hers. She might be content snuggling with a guy, but the guy's body is working at a much faster pace. Be honest with yourself and with each other, and make your resolutions clear. Men respond and work best when they have a concrete goal and they feel they are needed for a task. If it is clear to you that she trusts you in leading her toward God, it will be easier for you to rise to the challenge.

After your talk, sit there in church and write each other a love letter promising to lead one another to purity and to God. Vague resolutions do not stand well, so do not just say, "I promise to be more pure." This kind of resolution is worthless. Be specific. Exchange the letters, read them, and go buy a pair of chastity rings as a reminder of your commitment to God and to each other. (Tell your parents about this—I am sure your mom and dad would be more than willing to fork over some money for a chastity ring!) After buying the rings, go back to your place (with your parents or roommate home) and cook her dinner. I consider this romance without regret. By striving toward God together, you will find a unique bond that is known by few couples. In fact, married couples "who frequently pray together are twice as likely as those who pray less often to describe their marriages as highly romantic."[251]

Besides the chastity ring and love letter date, I recommend going on group dates, since you are less likely to get into tempting situations with good friends around you. Be careful about spending too much time alone. Even if you do not group date, people are so stuck on going to dinner and a movie that dates can get pretty monotonous. Get creative, and do some service work together for a change. Maybe the two of you could buy groceries, make lunches, and pass them out one by one to poor people downtown. If you are into sports, then try some sport together that you have never done.

The bottom line is to plan ahead for a date, especially if it will be in the evening. When a couple has not put any effort into making plans for a night, it is easier for boredom to set in and they may become sexually intimate since they can not think of anything else to do. Lastly—and perhaps most importantly—avoid those places where the two of you have fallen in the past. If you have a favorite scenic overlook, do not expect to drive there late at night with her and end up playing Scrabble. Likewise, avoid alcohol and drugs, since these are the gateway to many regrets.

I just rattled off a bunch of useful guidelines, but it is important to recognize that guidelines do not create purity of heart. They create a safer environment in which the virtue of purity can grow. The actual development of purity comes about through prayer. God reveals our calling and mission through prayer. This is essential for a guy, because the key to glorifying God in our relationships is to know what our task is with a girl. Some men go to great lengths to plan a night so that they say and do all the right things to get a woman to hop in bed with them. They know their goal, plan ahead, and achieve what they set out to do.

We Christian men have a great deal to learn from these guys— not in regard to their goal, but in regard to their focused determination. Before spending time with a young woman, we must have a premeditated agenda and deliberate plans . . . to bless the girl. Instead of being determined to take from the girl—to "get some" —we are called from the cross to empty ourselves, to direct our creativity, skill, and passion toward selfless love instead of selfish lust. Bluntly, God invites us to come and die. Or, as Christ said, "Whoever wishes to come after me must deny himself, take up his cross, and follow me" (Mark 8:34). It is through this emptying of ourselves that we find our manhood.

91

If you are on a date and things are going too far, how do you stop suddenly and tell him "no"?

Most situations of impurity can be avoided if you think ahead and avoid people and places that are likely to endanger your purity. But if you are already in a situation where you need to cool it off, there are a number of things you can say. Everyone seems to recommend different approaches.

For starters, do not underestimate the direct approach: Simply saying "We need to stop—we're going too far" may do the trick, especially if it is already understood that you are committed to chastity. Include yourself as well as him—say "*We* need to stop" instead of "*You* need to stop"—to indicate that you are not blaming him, just putting on the brakes. This may be hard, but consider it a learning experience so that you do not let things get to that point again.

On the other hand, some prefer the humorous approach: "Here is fifty cents. Call my dad, and if he says it's okay for us to do what you want, then I'll do it." Or, "You've got protection? Good. You are going to need it if you don't get your hands off me." And then there is, "Everyone's doing it? Then you shouldn't have trouble finding someone else."

These may be entertaining but I do not know how realistic they are. It might be more practical to give him a compliment—guys love that—such as, "I really like you, and I have so much fun when we're together, but this is the kind of stuff I want to save for marriage." Also, feel free to blame your parents for your decision: "My mom would kill me if she ever found out we were doing this. I need to cool off."

Another reason to skip the humorous approach is that this is not a time for jokes, but for witnessing to the truth of love. Be humble but clear, confident, and firm, and see this as a teachable moment. Use a verbal "no" *and* a "no" with your body language. If you are lying with him on a couch and whispering a half-hearted "no," he probably will not take you seriously, since you do not take your commitment to purity seriously. Also, when a girl is unable to say no, she is less attractive. Wendy Shalit described a "deadness" in girls' demeanor, "that comes from inauthenticity, from giving away too much," from not knowing how to set limits and having the character to stand by them.[252] To avoid this deadness, pray to God for the strength to maintain and grow in your purity.

Even if you do not convince your date to live purely in his own life, that is okay. It is more important that you do what is right than it is for you to convince another. You should not have to play the chastity cop. In fact, both people in a relationship should be mutually accountable. The responsibility to blow the whistle should not rest entirely on one person. Also, you do not owe your date a thirty-minute presentation on why chastity is important to you, and you certainly do not owe him sexual favors. If he does not accept a simple no, then he does not love you.

Let the guy go, and look for a man who knows how to honor a woman. Most important, do not be afraid. One teenage girl wrote to me and said, "I really like him, but I do not know why I have sex, like sometimes I am scared to say no." There are worse things in the world than not being asked out again by a guy who only loves himself. If he dumps you over this, then he did not deserve your attention to begin with. Could this be embarrassing? Perhaps. But regret lasts much longer than embarrassment.

It also might not be embarrassing at all. One high school girl said to me, "I know a lot of guys who act like they want sex just because they think they have to think that. But really, on the inside they are not like that at all." Sometimes it is a relief for a guy when a girl is clear about her boundaries and has strong values. It may take the pressure off a guy who assumes that you expect him to act like the rest of the guys. The numerous stories of sexual conquests that guys overhear in the locker room may make good guys think they are less of a man if they do not try to go as far with a woman as their classmates have. Men are sometimes afraid that a woman will think them unmanly or reject them if the men do not try to have sex with them. Your date may be trying to go too far with you in order to avoid appearing less of a man. Your character will serve to remind him of real manhood.

If it is too difficult to say no because the temptation is so strong, remember that you have the ability to tell your body what to do. It will obey you. If a married couple were having sex and their house caught on fire, do you think they would say, "Oh no! We can't say no to sex. We're going to die!"? Or do you think they would they stop their actions—no matter how intimate and exciting—and save their lives? In the same way, remember that you have the capacity to sacrifice the pleasures of the moment for a greater good—to save your spiritual life.

When things are going too far, value yourself enough to say no. Unfortunately, many young women use physical intimacy as a way of giving themselves value. The embraces feel like an affirmation of their worth, and perhaps because of mistakes they have made in the past, they do not understand the tremendous value of their bodies. Your purity is a treasure, so have the confidence to respect yourself. When the two of you work to preserve purity, it will keep an element of mystery and excitement in your relationship that is lost when couples do not bother to keep anything secret and sacred.

92

The life of chastity seems so hard. How am I supposed to resist with all the pressure out there from the other guys, and how do I tell my girlfriend that I want to be pure without feeling like a geek?

A heart filled with love rises to the greatest challenges. In college, I used to wake up at 5:00 in the morning twice a week to meet with the young woman I was seeing. Then we would drive to Pittsburgh in the freezing weather in order to do pro-life work together. I am not a morning person, and since I was born in Florida and raised in Arizona, I am not real big on snow either. But the sacrifice of getting up in the cold did not seem to matter because of the joy of being together. In the same way, the sacrifices you make to live chastely seem light when they are done for the sake of love.

When we lose sight of why we are sacrificing, the challenges of love seem heavy. You may be tempted to think, "No one's going to get hurt from a little fun on a date. Maybe I should just give in." That is when you must look into your heart and remember why—or more specifically, for whom—you are waiting. What is worth more: a few moments of pleasure or the lifelong joy that your bride will have knowing that you saved yourself for her? Always remember that love for a woman and the exercise of chastity go hand in hand. One cannot stand without the other. When it comes to love and lust, one will be in control. Either love will overpower lust and your passions will be under your control, or lust will dominate and corrupt any love that was once present. It is your choice.

I will admit that a life of chastity involves times of trial and even heroic struggle. This is because struggle can not be separated from love. The kind of love that endures and makes you happy is not easy. "Chastity is a difficult, long term matter," Pope John Paul II said. "One must wait patiently for it to bear fruit, for the happiness of loving kindness which it must bring. But at the same time, chastity is the sure way to happiness." [253] Did you catch that? Chastity is the sure way to happiness. Love can be demanding at times, but it is precisely because of that challenge that true love takes on such a rare beauty.

In regard to what to say to your girlfriend so that you do not feel like a geek, how about something along these lines: "I have so much fun when we're together, and I really like being with you . . . so I do not want to mess this up by doing things I know we will regret. I want to fall in love with you for all the right reasons."

Trust me, when you say that, "geek" will not be on her mind. But if she, or any of the guys, look down on you for having this much love, so be it. You care more about your God, the heart of your future spouse, and the health of your future children than you do about the passing pleasures of prom night and the opinions of an adolescent locker room. She is worth waiting for—even if you are the only one who seems to realize it. So wait for the woman God has in mind for you, and when you get married your bride can spend the entire honeymoon telling you how much of a geek she thinks you are for waiting for her. Sometimes being a geek is excessively romantic.

If others pressure you, some adults advise that you forget the insults and mockery. I advise the opposite. Remember the names that you are called for living a chaste life, and remember the jokes. Then when you stand before the altar and lift your bride's white veil, listen. Listen carefully. Where is the laughter? There is only silence, because you have won. You are the victor; the guys who mocked you would pay a million bucks to be in your shoes right now.

The bottom line is this: true love is such a great gift because it is so costly. As Mother Teresa said, "Love, to be real, it must cost—it must hurt—it must empty us of self."[254] It might even cost you your reputation with certain people, but this is precisely why true love is such a rarity today. Those who have the goal of true love should prepare their hearts for sacrifice. God knows the path is challenging, but he would not call us to this lifestyle without providing us the graces to live it.

Sure, the mockery is not fun while you are going through it, but think about why they are pressuring you. It is not because their lifestyle is so fulfilling and they want what is best for you, but because your life of chastity sets the standard high. This probably makes others feel guilty. Their consciences would bug them less if you made the same mistakes everyone else is making. Believe me, you are not missing out on anything by not having a series of broken sexual relationships.

Withstand the abuse also for the sake of men. You see, we guys have a reputation as jerks and we bear a particular responsibility for the many wounds caused to women. There is a certain balance of love between the sexes that needs to be restored. Pope John Paul II wrote: "A special responsibility rests with the man, as if it depended more on him whether this balance is maintained or broken, or even—if already broken—reestablished."[255]

So I commend you for being willing to stand for virtue when it is anything but popular.

You may feel you stick out in a bad way, but without self-mastery, we do not stick out at all. We become dull beasts and there is nothing unique about us. With purity, we can become radiant, clear, and alive with a uniqueness that women will not fail to see. Sin dulls our individuality, so if we wish to be most unique and most fully ourselves, we will find our identity in Christ. God and women are both searching for men with backbone. For God's sake, may we be such men. The world today desperately needs men who are not afraid to be gentlemen, men who understand what it means to be a man and are willing to take up that yoke of responsibility, men who will guard a woman instead of seeking ways to empty her of her innocence.

93

How do you control sex drives? They can be a real pain sometimes —for girls as well as guys!

Sexual desires are not bad. It is what we do with them that can be good or bad. Your body will do what you tell it to do, so here are some tips for training.

Step number one is prayer. Set a daily prayer time and stick to it. I also recommend the frequent reception of the sacraments, especially Mass and reconciliation. The Eucharist is the fountain of purity, so tap into that. Going to Mass will not take away all of your temptations, but it will give you the grace of charity. In the Eucharist, Christ gives himself fully to us so that we might give ourselves fully. This is the foundation of chastity, because love motivates us to live for others instead of for ourselves. Make time for daily Mass and go whenever possible. If there is a church in your area that has a eucharistic chapel, make frequent visits to Jesus there. In other words, make your life intensely eucharistic.

There are many sacraments, prayers, and devotions that can strengthen your life. For example, I also suggest that you pray a rosary every day. This takes only fifteen to twenty minutes, so set some time aside for that. Praying the stations of the cross is another source of tremendous power that people tend to overlook. For a simple prayer, quietly and devoutly say the names of Jesus, Mary, and Joseph. Turn to the Bible, because it is a great source of grace and consolation whenever we need it. For starters, read 1 Peter 5:6–10. Find a good spiritual director. As they say, "He who has himself as a guide has a fool for a disciple."

Besides prayer, do not place yourself in relationships or situations where you know mistakes will happen. Sometimes we march right into tempting situations and then blame God that the temptations were too strong to resist. Surround yourself with good friends, because as Paul said, "Bad company ruins good morals" (1 Cor. 15:33). We may have heard our parents say that before, but research backs it up: "Only 4 percent of young people whose friends were not sexually active were sexually active themselves. Amongst those whose friends WERE sexually active, the figure was 43 percent."[256]

If you watch MTV or vulgar sitcoms or you read *Cosmopolitan*, *Seventeen*, or other things that you know to be impure, get rid of them. Consider them love pollution. Also, avoid being idle. This is the chief means by which we end up falling into sin. Keep yourself occupied with friends, service work, sports, hobbies, and the like.

This all requires a determination for purity. But consider how people deny themselves to get the perfect body. If Americans spent one-tenth that time caring for their souls, we would be a nation of saints. No one thinks a man is repressive if he eats healthy food to prepare for a marathon. In the same way, what you are preparing for—love and holiness—requires serious training. You will not be repressing your sexual desires, but redirecting that energy toward selfless love.

Paul went through the same struggle. "For I do not do the good I want," he said, "but the evil I do not want is what I do . . .

but I see in my members another law at war with the law of my
mind and making me captive to the law of sin which dwells in
my members" (Rom. 7:19–23). During this struggle, remember
that God's grace is sufficient, for his power is made perfect in
our weakness (2 Cor. 12:9). Ask God for the wisdom to avoid
temptation and the grace to please him. He will give it to you. In
the words of a wise priest, "The one obstacle that can turn our
lives to misery is the refusal to believe that God will give us the
victory of perfect chastity."[257]

94

*I do not understand the deal with modesty. If a guy has a bad imag-
ination, that should be his issue and not mine. Why should I have
to dress a certain way for his sake?*

If you are fed up with the way guys often treat women and wonder what can be done to restore a sense of respect, modesty is
your number one weapon. The problem is this: Many men today do not know how to relate to women. Part of the remedy
for this ailment lies in the hands of women. Wendy Shalit said,
"Ultimately, it seems that only men can teach other men how
to behave around women, but those men have to be inspired by
women in the first place; inspired enough to think the women
are worth being courteous to."[258]

How will this happen? Well, many young women are aware
that they have the power to seduce a man, but few girls are aware
that their femininity also has the power to educate a guy. The
way a girl dresses (not to mention the way she talks, dances, and
so forth), has an extraordinary ability to help shape a man into a
gentleman or into a beast.

I have read tens of thousands of pages of theology and sex education, but I never learned how to treat a woman until I dated one
who dressed modestly. It was captivating, and I realized for the
first time that immodest dress gets in the way of seeing a woman

for who she is. Immodest outfits might attract a man to a girl's body, but it distracts him from seeing her as a person. As one man said, "If you want a man to respect you, and perhaps eventually fall in love with you, then you must show him that you respect yourself and that you recognize your dignity before God."[259]

A woman who dresses modestly inspires a guy in a way that I am not ashamed to admit I cannot explain. I suppose it is safe to say that it conveys your worth to us. When a woman dresses modestly, I can take her seriously as a woman because she is not preoccupied with clamoring for attention. Such humility is radiant. Unfortunately, many women are so preoccupied with turning men's heads that they overlook their power to turn our hearts.

Sometimes femininity is confused with weakness, but nothing could be further from the truth. A woman who is truly feminine is well aware that she could dress like a collection of body parts, and receive countless stares from guys. But she has the strength to leave more room for mystery. Instead of dressing in a way that invites guys to lust, the way she dresses says, "I'm worth waiting for." She trusts God's timing, and she knows that she does not need to make boys gawk in order to catch the attention of the man God has planned for her.

In his letter on the dignity of women, Pope John Paul II said: "The hour is coming, in fact has come, when the vocation of women is being acknowledged in its fullness, the hour in which women acquire in the world an influence, an effect and a power never hitherto achieved. That is why, at this moment when the human race is undergoing so deep a transformation, women imbued with a spirit of the Gospel can do so much to aid humanity in not falling."[260]

So what is modesty? It is not about looking as ugly as possible. It is about taking the natural beauty of womanhood, and adorning it in a way that adequately reflects her true identity. She is a daughter of the king of heaven, and her outfits, posture, and mannerisms do not distract from this. She is aware that her body is a temple of the Holy Spirit, and that her body is sacred. This brings about a certain humility of the body, since humility is the proper attitude toward greatness. In this case, it is the greatness of being made in the image and likeness of God.

This is not an "I am woman, hear me roar!" bit, but a serene sense of not needing to grope for attention. Sure, guys will gawk at a woman who dresses provocatively, but in your heart, do you long to be gawked at or to be loved? You want real love. When a girl dresses immodestly, she often does not realize that she robs herself of the intimacy for which she yearns. When a girl wears outfits that could not be any tighter without cutting off her circulation, she is telling guys: "Hey boys, the greatest thing about me is my body." They will stare, and will probably agree. If her body is the greatest thing about her, it must be all downhill from there. If that is the best she has to offer, then why should he get to know her heart, her dreams, her fears, and her family? He wants to get to know her body.

Dressing immodestly also harms a girl's chances of being loved. The type of guys who will be drawn to her will not be the type of guys who will treat her as a daughter of God. The way a girl dresses sends out an unspoken invitation for men to treat her the way she looks. For example, consider a magazine that I recently saw at an airport newsstand. On the cover was a woman wearing a short skirt that could be mistaken for a wide belt. Her airtight top was scarcely the size of an unfolded napkin, and in big bold letters across the cover was "Suzie (or whatever her name was—I don't remember) wants men to respect her!" I wished her the best of luck and walked on to my gate (after covering up the magazine with a few issues of *Oprah*. I consider this a corporal work of mercy—clothing the naked). Although a girl deserves respect no matter what she wears, a guy can tell how much a woman respects herself by how she is dressed. If she does not respect herself, the odds are that guys will follow her lead.

In the heart of a woman, there is no desire to be a sex object. Is there a desire to receive attention, affection, and love? Certainly. But is there a desire to be reduced to an object? No girl wants to

go there, but many do for the sake of receiving emotional gratification. When a girl puts on a bellybutton-showing, spaghetti
strap shirt, she is not thinking about how she hopes to lead men
to sin. She thinks, "The woman on the cover of the magazine
wore this, and it turns heads. So, if I wear it, guys will look at me.
Maybe I'll even meet a nice one." In other words, the woman's
deep motivation is the desire to be loved.

Assume that a girl dresses provocatively and she comes across
a genuinely good man. The man is no better off because of her
outfit. Men are more visually stimulated than women, and im-
modesty can easily trigger lustful thoughts. When men harbor
these impure ideas, lust separates us from Christ, the source of
unconditional love. Does a woman really want to separate men
from the source of the unconditional love that she seeks? If not,
then why not opt for the more modest outfit? There is nothing
wrong with wearing things that make you look cute, but as a
Christian woman, seductive and sexy outfits should not be part
of your wardrobe. If your heart is saying, "Is this too short?"
or "Does this look too tight?" listen to that voice. It has already
answered your question.

Listen to this voice for your sake and for ours. For your sake,
realize that as a moat surrounds a castle, modesty protects the treasure of chastity. For our sake, remember when Cain killed Abel
back in Genesis? When God asked Cain where his brother was,
Cain replied, "Am I my brother's keeper?" In the same way, it is
all too easy for guys and girls alike to shrug off the responsibility
we have to help one another maintain purity. We need to adopt
the attitude of Paul, and live in a way that does not cause our
brother to stumble (Rom. 14:21).

Some girls spend more energy trying to make guys notice them
(even if they have no interest in the guys) than they spend trying
to focus young men's attention on God. As a woman of God, use
the beauty of modesty to inspire men to virtue. There is no problem with looking cute. Problems arise, however, when clothing
(or the lack thereof) is worn in a way that is immodest, or when

a person falls into vanity and excessive concern about looking perfect. Your body is precious in the sight of God, and you do not need to look like a *Cosmo* model to deserve love.

95

Is it bad to always be thinking sexual stuff about girls? If it is, what am I supposed to do?

To begin with, your sexual attraction toward women has been stamped into your heart by God, not by the devil. There is nothing sinful about being sexually attracted to a girl. It is normal and healthy. Do not feel guilty about sexual attraction because it is not the same thing as lust. Just because you have strong desires, this does not mean that you are impure.

Lust is a different matter because it is a conscious act of the will to allow your mind to imagine illicit sexual acts. Lust treats the person as an object—a thing to be used for your pleasure. Therefore, it is a distortion of love, and it will never satisfy. Illicit sexual acts such as premarital sex—or imagining premarital sex —are always incomplete.

Jesus wants us to have the fullness of love, and not sell ourselves short with lust, so he warned us that whoever looks lustfully at a woman has already committed adultery with her in his heart (Matt. 5:28). By saying this, Jesus is not condemning us but is calling us. Work as Paul did, to "take every thought captive to obey Christ" (2 Cor. 10:5).

In regard to what to do with tempting thoughts, I recommend what I have recommended elsewhere: If you have impure magazines, videos, and music, get rid of them. Become a man of prayer. Be patient with yourself. Impure thoughts are bound to come. Take it one day at a time, one minute at a time, and one thought at a time. Do not get overwhelmed. Purity of heart does not mean that you are never tempted and that you cease to be sexually attracted to others. Some people even think that they are pure just

202 IF YOU REALLY LOVED ME

because they do not have strong desires, or because they have never had the opportunity to be impure. This is not purity.

All that God asks is that you be faithful to him as he reveals himself to you in the present moment. He loves you and will give you the grace you need to keep purity as something beautiful for God. As you grow in control over your mind, you will have greater and greater control over your body. "No temptation has overtaken you that is not common to man. God is faithful, and he will not let you be tempted beyond your strength, but with the temptation will also provide the way of escape, that you may be able to endure it" (1 Cor. 10:13).

96

How can I promote this message of chastity at my school?

I would recommend three things. First, pray and fast for your school. In the Gospel of Mark, Jesus spoke about how some people could only be healed of their spiritual illness through other people praying and fasting for them (9:29).

Second, one of the most effective things you can do to spread the message of chastity is to live it. This is because the virtue of purity is more easily caught than taught. As St. Francis said, "Preach the gospel always. When necessary, use words." Your silent example comes first. If you are in a dating relationship, make sure that God is the center of it so that your classmates will see what joy a godly relationship can bring. Even if you are not dating anyone, your witness of purity is just as powerful. "Let no one despise your youth, but set the believers an example in speech and conduct, in love, in faith, in purity" (1 Tim. 4:12).

The world seriously doubts that chastity can exist in the lives and relationships of modern couples. It refuses to believe that two young people madly in love with one another can resist temptation. What the world does not see is that as long as the couple has a motive—true love—it is very possible. Not only is it possible, Mary Beth Bonacci observed that couples who live chastity "were having an easier time getting out of bad relationships. They were making better marriage decisions. They were happier."[261]

Therefore, be a light to the world. Your school needs to see that we do not embrace chastity for the sake of avoiding infection or unwanted pregnancy.

Everyone is aware of the sexual messages that bombard us on every television channel and radio station. The message of "sexual liberation" surrounds us. Unfortunately, to curb this permissiveness, the message of purity has often been couched in terms like "just say *no*," "true love *waits*," "*abstain*." All of these slogans can create the impression that purity is nothing more than a system of restraints. It does not appeal to a person who only knows the immediate "love" and affection of purely physical relationships. Because of this, the message of chastity needs to be rehabilitated so that everyone will be able to see the clear and obvious link between true love, total freedom, and purity. It is not about avoiding venereal infection. It is about having a better kind of love.

One girl said after hearing a talk on sexual purity, "I agree with everything you say. I know most of my friends would, too. It all makes so much sense. It's just that no one else I know is actually doing it. I don't know if I'm strong enough to be the first one. Maybe if a group of us all started together."[262] This is your job —to create a culture in which it is easy to be good, a climate favorable to purity. In the words of Catherine of Siena, "If you are what you should be, you will set the world on fire."[263]

I I

Vocations

97

How do I know if God is calling me to be a priest, or get married, or whatever?

Some people hear the call to religious life when they are in first grade. Others seem to receive the call after they have spent a decade in a professional career. Each calling is a bit different. But whether you hope to get married, ordained, or live a life offered to God through religious vows, all are ways of serving God. Some also serve God in the single life. We can know what God is calling us to if we learn to listen to him.

Here are several things that you can do to listen to him. Set a daily prayer time and stick to it. To hear God's calling, you must listen. To listen to God, we must learn to pray. To learn to pray, we must make time to pray and ask the Holy Spirit to teach us how. Listening to him involves patience and obedience, so be still in your prayer time and allow God to speak in the silence of your heart. This takes practice, but like any good relationship it will deepen according to how much effort you put into it. Sin damages this relationship, so work toward holiness. Though we may not associate chastity with discernment, it is an essential virtue if we hope to hear our calling. When a young man or woman is indulging in sexual sin, the mind seems to be filled with such dull and heavy thoughts that he or she is unable to recognize the voice of God.

Also, it is wise to find a holy priest who can act as your spiritual director. He has probably been listening to God's voice since before you were born, so you can benefit from his sanctity. Also speak about your vocation with people whose holiness and joy you admire. Pope John Paul II advises: "In the first place I say this: you must never think that you are alone in deciding your future! And second: when deciding your future, you must not decide for yourself alone!. . ."[264] "Confidently open your most intimate aspirations to the love of Christ who waits for you in the Eucharist. You will receive the answer to all your worries and you will see with joy that the consistency of your life which he asks of you is the door to fulfill the noblest dreams of your youth. . . ."[265] "The search and discovery of God's will for you is a deep and fascinating endeavor. Every vocation, every path to which Christ calls us, ultimately leads to fulfillment and happiness, because it leads to God, to sharing in God's own life."[266]

If you are considering the priesthood, it is beneficial to spend some time on a good discernment retreat, if one is available. One other method of discernment is to reflect on your life: look at what doors the Lord has opened or shut in your life, look at what talents he has given you, and what desires he has placed on your heart. Often, we complicate the discernment process more than we need to, and we lose our peace. Whatever vocation God calls you to, this will be the place where you will have the most joy. Each vocation will have plenty of suffering as well, but all are ways that you can become holy.

During this time of discernment, be patient. At times, God does not want us to know his will. That may sound strange, but we grow in the times where he seems silent. His will is our holiness, and trusting in him during this time of uncertainty may be all he is calling you to right now. In the meantime, I recommend that you pray one Hail Mary each day for your vocation. May our Lady guide you to hear the voice of her Son and give you the courage to respond generously. In the words of Pope John Paul II, "My desire is for the young people of the entire world to come closer to Mary. She is the bearer of an indelible youthfulness and beauty that never wanes. May young people have increasing confidence in her and may they entrust the life just opening before them to her."[267]

98

I am going to a university in the fall and I am setting my heart on meeting someone there. If not, I think I may have to become a lay celibate. Is this being too harsh on myself?

I would not plan on taking a religious vow of celibacy through your bishop if you do not meet the right person within your time frame. When we try to force our vocation into a timetable, we are acting out of impatience and saying to God, "You've got X amount of months to accomplish my will." Often, God's ways are not our ways, so pray that God will make it clear if he calls you to the celibate life. If you accept any vocation, it should be out of generosity, love, and courage, not frustration.

Sometimes we decide what we want in order to be happy, and then we wait until we get it to become pleased with life. This is a recipe for unhappiness, because God gives us what we need, not always what we want. Though this time of singleness may seem like a problem, perhaps you need to look at it differently. Mother Teresa used to say that there are no problems in life. There are only challenges in love for Jesus. She also remarked that the world sees everything as a "problem." Why not use the word "gift?"

Why a gift? Well, the vocation that God has in mind for you is where you will have the most joy. You do not want a marriage that he has not willed, and you do not want to have a marriage before God wills it. In the words of the Song of Songs, "stir not up nor awaken love until it please" (Song 3:5). You may feel that love's time is long overdue, but trust that the Lord will act and know that his timing is perfect.

Take one day at a time. His faithfulness and kindness reach to the skies, and God has glory in what he conceals. He wants you where you are right now, and embracing his will as it is given to you in the present moment is a great means to sanctity. Also, remember that a vocation is not the ultimate purpose for our existence. Holiness is. God may not be calling you to a vocation today, but he is calling you to holiness.

I understand that this time of loneliness is difficult, but allow the words of Scripture to console you and encourage you to persevere:

> My son, if you come forward to serve the Lord, prepare yourself for temptation. Set your heart right and be steadfast, and do not be hasty in time of calamity. Cleave to him and do not depart, that you may be honored at the end of your life. Accept whatever is brought upon you, and in changes that humble you be patient. For gold is tested in the fire, and acceptable men in the furnace of humiliation. Trust in him, and he will help you; make your ways straight, and hope in him. . . . Consider the ancient generations and see: who ever trusted in the Lord and was put to shame? . . . For the Lord is compassionate and merciful (Sir. 2:1–6, 10, 11).

99

I have thought about the priesthood or religious life, but I can't imagine not having sex at least once my whole life. Wouldn't God understand if I had it once for the sake of experiencing it?

To choose celibacy is to offer the gift of your sexuality to God. Notice, by the way, that we only offer to God things that are good, not things that are bad or sinful. In ancient Israel, only the best lambs or the firstfruits of the harvest were fit to be offered as sacrifices; the prophets warned that God did not look kindly on those who offered crippled or sickly beasts, especially if they were holding back the better animals (see Mal. 1:6–14).

Likewise, your sexuality is a precious gift, and there is nothing more beautiful you can do with it than to offer it up to God. Would you really want to cheapen that gift? Which would you prefer: to be able to offer God the pure and unblemished gift of your virginity, or to seize the "firstfruits" for yourself, in the process defiling both yourself and another, and then offering God the leftovers?

In the same way that a man who is planning on getting married and becoming a father suddenly begins reevaluating his life in light of the responsibilities and expectations of fatherhood, so a young person thinking about the priesthood or religious life should be thinking about living up to God's expectations—not living down to the expectations of the world.

Yes, this is demanding; Jesus demands that *all* his followers be ready to make sacrifices: "No one who puts his hand to the plow and looks back is fit for the kingdom of God" (Luke 9:62). Persevere for Christ. "Stand by your covenant and attend to it, and grow old in your work. Do not wonder at the works of a sinner, but trust in the Lord and keep at your toil; for it is easy in the sight of the Lord to enrich a poor man quickly and suddenly" (Sir. 11:20-21).

Do not make the mistake of thinking about celibacy in negative terms. If you become a priest or religious, then the gift of your sexuality will be given to God. It is not being wasted, but you are being offered as a living sacrifice, holy and acceptable to the Lord. As Pope John Paul II said, young people "know that their life has meaning to the extent that it becomes a free gift for others."[268] Your entire life and body will become a total gift to God. If he has called you to himself, then you are his. Your life is to be hidden with Christ in God. Your gift is meant for him, and to give it away to another would be like a bride giving her virginity away to a stranger the night before her wedding. Make this sacrifice for God, as a bride waits for her groom.

As a reward for such a generous donation of self, Christ promises, "There is no one who has left house or brothers or sisters or mother or father or children or lands, for my sake and for the gospel, who will not receive a hundredfold now in this time, houses and brothers and sisters and mothers and children and lands, with persecutions, and in the age to come eternal life" (Mark 10:29-30).

Also, remember that the marital act is only a sign that points to the eternal reality. The celibacy of Catholic priests around the world is a constant witness to humanity that there is a greater reality than the daily affairs and pleasures of earth. By giving up marital intercourse in this life, you are essentially saying to God that you are skipping the sign and beginning to embrace the reality of total union with God.

100

Don't you think that the vocations crisis would be over if priests could be married?

This is a good question, and the answer may be a bit surprising. The Vatican has essentially declared that the vocations crisis is over. It reported in 1997 that "In 1978 there were 63,882 seminarians; at present there are 108,517, an increase of 69.87 percent. The increase in Africa and Asia, in fact, is incredible. Over the last twenty years, these two continents have seen an increase of 238.50 percent and 124.01 percent respectively."[269] Over the past twenty years, vocations have increased on every continent around the globe. In America, the number of seminarians has increased from 22,000 to 35,000 in the last two decades. In fact, vocations today are flourishing in dioceses where traditional Catholic teaching is presented in its fullness.

Would the number of vocations be even greater if married men could be ordained? There is no empirical evidence for this. For example, Eastern Orthodox churches (which allow priests to be married) are not experiencing any greater increase in vocations. Historically, the discipline of priestly celibacy has been with us from the beginning. Although this is not an unchangeable aspect of the priesthood—it is a Church discipline that the Church has the authority to change if it sees fit—I would not look for the change to come. Celibacy is an enormous blessing to the Church, not a burden. It allows priests to serve Christ and his flock in ways that otherwise would be impossible. The Church has decided to maintain this discipline rooted in the example and the teaching of Jesus and Paul.

Paul advocates celibacy on the grounds that it enables people to devote their lives exclusively to serving God in prayer and service to the world, whereas marriage limits their ability to devote themselves to those things (1 Cor. 7). Likewise, Jesus speaks of "those who have renounced marriage for the sake of the kingdom of heaven." A more literal translation refers to those who have "made themselves eunuchs for the sake of the kingdom of heaven" (Matt. 19:11–12). The term he uses refers to a celibate royal servant who was in charge of taking care of a king's wives. In the same way, priests have embraced consecrated virginity in order to care for the Church, the bride of Christ—the King of Kings.

I think that a vocations crisis is not the result of abstinence among clergy, but of an absence of the virtue of chastity within families. In the words of one Church document, "A lack of vocations follows from the breakdown of the family, yet where parents are generous in welcoming life, children will be more likely to be generous when it comes to the question of offering themselves to God."[270] I also believe that our lack of prayerfulness is to blame for the lack of priests in some areas. Jesus told us to ask the harvest master to send out laborers to gather his harvest (Matt. 9:38). Have we?

Resources

Birth Control Pill: Side Effects and Alternatives

Kahlenborn, Chris, M.D. *Breast Cancer: Its Link to Abortion and the Birth Control Pill*. Dayton, Ohio: One More Soul, 2000.

Wilks, John B., Pharm. M.P.S. *A Consumer's Guide to the Pill and Other Drugs*. Stafford, Virginia: American Life League, 1997.

Pope Paul VI Institute for the Study of Human Reproduction: web site: www.popepaulvi.com phone: (402) 390-6600

Catholic Faith

Bonacci, Mary Beth. *We're on a Mission from God*. San Francisco: Ignatius Press, 1996.

Pinto, Matt. *Did Adam and Eve have Belly-Buttons?* New Hope, Kentucky: Ascension Press, 1998.

Catechism of the Catholic Church. San Francisco: Ignatius Press, 1994.

Pillar of Fire, Pillar of Truth. San Diego: Catholic Answers, 1998.

Catholic Answers: web site: www.catholic.com phone: (619) 387-7200

Nazareth Research Library: www.jimmyakin.com

Cohabitation

All About Cohabiting Before Marriage: www.members.aol.com/cohabiting

Contraception

Smith, Janet. "Contraception, Why Not." Audiotape: (888) 291-8000

Crisis Pregnancy

The Nurturing Network: (800) 866-4666

Homosexuality

Harvey, John. *The Truth about Homosexuality: The Cry of the Faithful*. San Francisco: Ignatius Press, 1996.

Courage: web site: www.couragerc.net phone: (212) 421-1426

National Association for Research and Therapy of Homosexuality: web site: www.narth.com phone (818) 789-4440

Internet Filters

Kids Online: www.protectkids.com

Familyclick: www.familyclick.com

Love and Relationships

Bonacci, Mary Beth. *Real Love*. San Francisco: Ignatius Press, 1996.

Evert, Jason. *Pure Love*. San Diego: Catholic Answers, 1999.

Wojtyla, Karol (Pope John Paul II). *Love and Responsibility*. San Francisco: Ignatius Press, 1993.

Catholic Answers' chastity information:
www.catholic.com/chastity

National Abstinence Clearinghouse: www.abstinence.net

Louisiana Governor's Program on Abstinence:
www.abstinencedu.com

Marriage

Sheen, Fulton. *Three to Get Married*. Princeton, New Jersey: Scepter Publishers, 1951.

West, Christopher. *Good News about Sex and Marriage*. Ann Arbor, Michigan: Servant Publications, 2000.

West, Christopher. Audiotapes of presentations on marriage and human sexuality. Our Father's Will Communications: (252) 429-9266

Natural Family Planning

Kippley, John, and Sheila Kippley. *The Art of Natural Family Planning*. Cincinnati, Ohio: The Couple to Couple League, 1982.

Couple to Couple League: web site: www.ccli.org phone: (800) 745-8252

Pope Paul VI Institute for the Study of Human Reproduction: web site: www.popepaulvi.com phone: (402) 390-6600

Overpopulation Myth

Kasun, Jacqueline. *The War Against Population: The Economics and Ideology of World Population Control*. San Francisco: Ignatius Press, 1988, 1999.

Kasun, Jacqueline. "Too Many People?" *Envoy*, May–June 1998, 32–37.

Population Research Institute: www.pop.org

Post-Abortion Help

Project Rachel: (800) 593-2273

Sexual Temptations

Arteburn, Stephen, and Fred Stoeker. *Every Young Man's Battle*. Colorado Springs, Colorado: WaterBrook Press, 2002.

Pure Intimacy (Focus on the Family): www.pureintimacy.com

Sexually Transmitted Diseases (STD)

Wilson, Mercedes Arzú. *Love & Family*. San Francisco: Ignatius Press, 1996.

Wetzel, Richard, M.D. *Sexual Wisdom*. Ann Arbor, Michigan: Proctor Publications, 1998.

Medical Institute for Sexual Health: www.medinstitute.org

Focus on the Family: www.family.org

STD Testing

America's Crisis Pregnancy Helpline: (800) 672-2296

Notes

[1] Pope John Paul II, address, Vigil of Prayer, Tor Vergata, Rome, World Youth Day, 19 August 2000.

[2] Pope John Paul II, address, Message of the Holy Father to the Youth of the World, Vatican, World Youth Day, 29 June 1999.

INTRODUCTION

[3] *Sex and Disease: What You Need to Know* (New York: Planned Parenthood Federation of America, 1988). As quoted by Richard Wetzel, M.D., *Sexual Wisdom* (Ann Arbor, Michigan: Proctor Publications, L.L.C., 1998), 57 (emphasis mine).

[4] Sharon Begley, "Sex and the Single Fly," *Newsweek*, 14 August 2000, 44–45.

[5] *Cosmopolitan*, September 2001, cover.

[6] Pope John Paul II, encyclical letter, *Redemptor Hominis* 10 (The Redeemer of Man), (Boston: Pauline Books & Media, 1979).

CHASTITY AND THE MEANING OF SEX

[7] Wendy Shalit, *A Return to Modesty* (New York: Touchstone, 1999), 193.

[8] Proverbs 25:2.

[9] William Mattox Jr., "Aha! Call It the Revenge of the Church Ladies," *USA Today*, 11 February 1999 (www.usatoday.com).

[10] Edward O. Laumann, John H. Gagnon, Robert T. Michael, and Stuart Michaels, *The Social Organization of Sexuality: Sexual Practices in the United States* (Chicago: University of Chicago Press, 1994), 1. As quoted by Glenn T. Stanton, *Why Marriage Matters* (Colorado Springs, Colorado: Piñon Press, 1997), 41.

[11] Laumann and others, *The Social Organization of Sexuality*, table 10.5, 364. As quoted by Stanton, *Why Marriage Matters*, 41.

[12] Laumann and others, *The Social Organization of Sexuality*, table 10.7, 368. As quoted by Stanton, *Why Marriage Matters*, 41.

[13] W. R. Mattox, "What's Marriage Got to Do with It? Good Sex Comes to Those Who Wait," *Family Policy* 6:6 (1994): 1–8. As quoted by Wetzel, *Sexual Wisdom*, 23.

¹⁴ Winnifred B. Cutler, *Love Cycles: The Science of Intimacy* (New York: Villard Books, 1991), 108–109, 244. As quoted by Stanton, *Why Marriage Matters*, 46.

¹⁵ Les Parrott III and Leslie Parrott, *Saving Your Marriage Before It Starts* (Grand Rapids, Michigan: Zondervan Publishing House, 1995), 145.

¹⁶ Elisabeth Elliot, *Passion and Purity* (Grand Rapids, Michigan: Revell, 1984), 21.

¹⁷ *Catechism of the Catholic Church* 2339 (San Francisco: Ignatius Press, 1994).

¹⁸ True Love Waits, "Interview with a Non-virgin," 15 April 2001 (www.lifeway.com/tlw/tns_adv_wjjarc.asp).

¹⁹ Josh McDowell, *Why Wait?* (Nashville, Tennessee: Nelson Book Publishers, 1987), 16.

²⁰ J. D. Teachman, J. Thomas, and K. Paasch, "Legal Status and the Stability of Coresidential Unions," *Demography* (November 1991): 571–583. As quoted by Christopher West, *Good News About Sex and Marriage* (Ann Arbor, Michigan: Servant Publications, 2000), 71.

²¹ Thomas Lickona, "Sex, Love, and Character: It's Our Decision" (address given to assembly of students at Seton Catholic High School, Binghamton, New York, 8 January 1999), 10.

²² All About Cohabiting Before Marriage, "Myths about Cohabitation" (www.members.aol.com/cohabiting/myths.htm).

²³ R. A. Hatcher and others, *Contraceptive Technology*, 1994, 515. As reported by Westside Pregnancy Resource Center, "Teen Sex and Pregnancy: Facts and Figures," 29 March 2002 (www.w-cpc.org/sexuality/teens.html).

²⁴ As reported by D. P. Orr, M. Beiter, G. Ingersoll, "Premature Sexual Activity as an Indicator of Psychological Risk," *Pediatrics* 87 (February 1991): 141–147. As quoted by "Building Healthy Futures," *Sexual Health Update* (Special Supplement): 1.

²⁵ *Neural Oxytocinergic Systems as Genomic Targets for Hormones and as Modulators of Hormone-Dependant Behaviors* (New York: Rockefeller University, 1999). As quoted by Eric J. Keroack, M.D. and John R. Diggs Jr., M.D., "Bonding Imperative," A Special Report from the Abstinence Medical Council. As quoted by Abstinence Clearinghouse, 30 April 2001.

²⁶ Keroack and Diggs, "Bonding Imperative."

²⁷ See also Romans 1:18, 6:12–14; 1 Corinthians 6:9–11; 2 Corinthians 7:1; Galatians 5:16–23; Ephesians 4:17–24, 5:3–13; Colossians 3:5–8; 1 Timothy 4:12.

²⁸ John 14:23–24.

²⁹ Thomas Lickona, "The Neglected Heart," *American Educator* (Summer 1994): 37–38.

³⁰ Jacqueline Jackson Kikuchi, Rhode Island Rape Crisis Center, Provi-

dence, Rhode Island. As quoted by *Harper's*, July 1988, 15. As quoted by Wetzel, *Sexual Wisdom*, 31.

³¹ Henry Cloud and John Townsend, *Boundaries in Dating* (Grand Rapids, Michigan: Zondervan, 2000), 252.

³² Mother Teresa, as quoted by www.motherteresa.com.

³³ Pope John Paul II, address, 18 May 1988, Asuncion, Paraguay. As quoted by Pedro Beteta López, ed., *The Meaning of Vocation* (Princeton, New Jersey: Scepter Publishers, 1997), 18–19.

³⁴ Pope John Paul II, address, 22 November 1986, Auckland, New Zealand. As quoted by López, ed., *The Meaning of Vocation*, 19.

³⁵ Pope John Paul II, address, 1 October 1979, Boston, Massachusetts, United States. As quoted by López, ed., *The Meaning of Vocation*, 19–20.

³⁶ West, *Good News About Sex and Marriage*, 29.

³⁷ The Consortium of State Physicians Resource Councils, "The Declines in Adolescent Pregnancy, Birth, and Abortion Rates in the 1990's: What Factors Are Responsible?" 7 January 1999, 5.

³⁸ Roper Starch Worldwide poll for The Sexuality Information and Education Council of the United States [SIECUS], 1994. As quoted by Mary Beth Bonacci, *Real Love* (San Francisco: Ignatius Press, 1996), 273–274. Also see *Seventeen* Magazine, May 1996.

DATING AND COURTSHIP

³⁹ Karol Wojtyla (Pope John Paul II), *Love and Responsibility* (San Francisco: Ignatius Press, 1993), 131.

⁴⁰ McDowell, *Why Wait?*, 110.

⁴¹ Joyce L. Vedral, *Boyfriends: Getting Them, Keeping Them, Living Without Them* (New York: Ballantine Books, 1990). As quoted by www.lovematters.com/teenstalk.htm.

⁴² Brent C. Miller, Terrence D. Olsen (Utah State University, Brigham Young University). As reported by McDowell, *Why Wait?*, 79.

⁴³ Eric and Leslie Ludy, *When God Writes Your Love Story* (Sisters, Oregon. Loyal Publishing, 1999), 64.

⁴⁴ St. Thérèse of Lisieux, *The Story of a Soul* (Rockford, Illinois: TAN Books and Publishers, Inc., 1997), 2.

⁴⁵ Elliot, *Passion and Purity*, 145.

⁴⁶ Dannah Gresh, *And the Bride Wore White* (Chicago: Moody Press, 1999), 70.

⁴⁷ Anthony Stern, M.D., ed., *Everything Starts from Prayer* (Ashland, Oregon: White Cloud Press, 1998), 130.

⁴⁸ Canadian Broadcasting Corporation interview with Mother Teresa.

[49] R. Allen Jackson. As quoted by the "Ask the Experts" forum of www.abstinencedu.com (2000).

[50] Lickona, "The Neglected Heart," 37.

[51] McDowell, *Why Wait?*, 16.

[52] Cloud and Townsend, *Boundaries in Dating*, 46.

[53] Ludy, *When God Writes Your Love Story*, 109.

[54] All About Cohabiting Before Marriage, "Sociological Reasons" (www.members.aol.com/cohabiting/soc.htm).

[55] Wojtyla (Pope John Paul II), *Love and Responsibility*, 171, emphasis added.

[56] Pope John Paul II, general audience, 3 December 1980. As quoted by *Theology of the Body* (Boston: Pauline Books & Media, 1997), 177.

[57] Wojtyla (Pope John Paul II), *Love and Responsibility*, 172.

[58] McDowell, *Why Wait?*, 17–18.

[59] Cloud and Townsend, *Boundaries in Dating*, 251.

[60] Laura Morgan, *Marie Claire*, 2000. As re-published by "How Strong is Your Sex Drive?" *Complete Woman*, February–March 2001, 17.

[61] Shalit, *A Return to Modesty*, 97.

[62] "Break-up Predictors," *Reader's Digest*, April 2002, 185.

[63] Cloud and Townsend, *Boundaries in Dating*, 228.

[64] McDowell, *Why Wait?*, 63.

PREPARING FOR MARRIAGE

[65] For financial advice before (and during) marriage, see Philip Lenahan, *The Catholic Answers Guide to Family Finances* (San Diego: Catholic Answers, 2000).

[66] Marcel Maciel, Mexico City, 12 March 1988.

[67] Wojtyla (Pope John Paul II), *Love and Responsibility*, 134.

[68] Parrott, *Saving Your Marriage Before It Starts*, 68.

[69] C. S. Lewis, *The Four Loves* (San Diego: Harcourt Brace & Company, 1960, 1988).

[70] Parrott, *Saving Your Marriage Before It Starts*, 41.

[71] Letter from Karol Wojtyla (Pope John Paul II) to Teresa Heydel, December 1956. As quoted by George Weigel, *Witness to Hope* (New York: Cliff Street Books, 2001), 101.

[72] John Paul II, homily, "The Love Within Families," 8 April 1982. As quoted by West, *Good News About Sex and Marriage*, 65.

[73] James Dobson, *Love Must Be Tough* (Dallas, Texas: Word Publishing, 1996), 209–213.

[74] William G. Axinn and Arland Thornton, "The Relation Between Cohab-

itation and Divorce: Selectivity or Casual Influence?" *Demography* 29 (1992): 357–374. As quoted by Stanton, *Why Marriage Matters*, 57.

[75] Larry L. Bumpass and James A. Sweet, "Cohabitation, Marriage, and Union Stability: Preliminary Findings from NSFH2 [National Survey of Families and Households]" (NSFH Working Paper No. 65, Center for Demography and Ecology, University of Wisconsin-Madison, 1995).

[76] Kim Camplisson, "Celebrating Christian Marriage," *The Southern Cross* (newspaper of the Diocese of San Diego), 26 April 2001, 8.

[77] Katherine A. London and Joan R. Kahn, "Premarital Sex and the Risk of Divorce," *Journal of Marriage and Family* 53 (1991): 845–855.

[78] Elizabeth Thompson and Ugo Colella, "Cohabitation and Marital Stability: Quality or Commitment?" *Journal of Marriage and the Family* 54 (1992): 263. As quoted by Stanton, *Why Marriage Matters*, 57; John D. Cunningham and John K. Antill, "Cohabitation and Marriage: Retrospective and Predictive Consequences," *Journal of Social and Personal Relationships* 11 (1994): 90. As quoted by Stanton, *Why Marriage Matters*, 58.

[79] Koray Tanfer and Renata Forste, "Sexual Exclusivity Among Dating, Cohabiting, and Married Women," *Journal of Marriage and Family* (February 1996): 33–47.

[80] Chuck Colson, "Trial Marriages on Trial: Why They Don't Work," *Breakpoint*, 20 March 1995.

[81] Lee Robins and Darrell Regier, *Psychiatric Disorders in America: The Epidemiologic Catchment Area Study* (New York: Free Press, 1991), 64. As quoted by Stanton, *Why Marriage Matters*, 66–67.

[82] Marianne K. Hering, "Believe Well, Live Well," *Focus on the Family*, September 1994, 4.

[83] William Mattox Jr., "Could This be True Love? Test It with Courtship, Not Cohabitation," *USA Today*, 10 February 2000, 15A (www.usatoday.com).

[84] Thompson and Colella, "Cohabitation and Marital Stability," 266. As quoted by Stanton, *Why Marriage Matters*, 57.

[85] G. K. Chesterton, *What's Wrong with the World* (San Francisco: Ignatius Press, 1910, 1994), 64.

[86] Wojtyla (Pope John Paul II), *Love and Responsibility*, 135.

[87] Teachman and Paasch, "Legal Status and the Stability of Coresidential Unions," 571–583. As quoted by West, *Good News About Sex and Marriage*, 71.

[88] See "Sexual Exclusivity Among Dating, Cohabiting, and Married Women," *Journal of Marriage and the Family* 58 (1996): 33–47. As quoted by West, *Good News About Sex and Marriage*, 72.

[89] *Catechism of the Catholic Church* 2350.

[90] Elliot, *Passion and Purity*, 179.

HOW FAR IS TOO FAR?

[91] Elliot, *Passion and Purity*, 131.

[92] Karen S. Peterson, "Younger Kids Trying It Now, Often Ignorant of Disease Risks," *USA Today*, 16 November 2000, 1D (www.usatoday.com).

[93] McDowell, *Why Wait?*, 115.

[94] Pope John Paul II, address, 29 April 1989, Antananarivo, Madagascar. As quoted by López, ed., *The Meaning of Vocation*, 28.

[95] Tom and Judy Lickona, *Sex, Love & You* (Notre Dame, Indiana: Ave Maria Press, 1994), 74.

[96] McDowell, *Why Wait?*, 172.

[97] Leon Kass, "The End of Courtship," *Public Interest* (Winter 1997). As quoted by Tom Lickona, "Sex, Character, and the College Culture: The Neglected Issue," (Institute on College Student Values, The Florida State University, 7 February 1998, photocopy), 6–7.

[98] "Dating Game," *Complete Woman*, 84.

PORNOGRAPHY AND MASTURBATION

[99] Wetzel, *Sexual Wisdom*, 72.

[100] West, *Good News About Sex and Marriage*, 84.

[101] U.S. Department of Justice. *Child Pornography, Obscenity, and Organized Crime*. Washington, D.C., February 1988.

[102] Laurie Hall, "When Fantasy Meets Reality" (www.pureintimacy.org/online1/essays/a0000006.html).

[103] Pope John Paul II, general audience, 24 November 1982. As quoted by *Theology of the Body*, 346.

[104] Pope John Paul II, apostolic letter, *Mulieris Dignitatem* 14 (On the Dignity and Vocation of Women), (Boston: Pauline Books & Media, 1988).

[105] C. S. Lewis, *The Great Divorce* (New York: MacMillan Publishing Company, 1946). As quoted by Gresh, *And the Bride Wore White*, 40.

[106] Douglas Weiss, M.D., *The Final Freedom* (Fort Worth, Texas: Discovery Press, 1998).

[107] Keroack and Diggs, "Bonding Imperative."

HOMOSEXUALITY

[108] R. McKie, "The Myth of the Gay Gene," *The Press* NZ, 30 July 1993, 9. As quoted by Neil and Briar Whitehead, *My Genes Made Me Do It!* (Lafayette, Louisiana: Huntington House Publishers, 1999), 135.

[109] W. Byne and B. Parsons, "Human Sexual Orientation: The Biological Theories Reappraised," *Archives of General Psychiatry* 50 (1993): 228–239;

"Gay Genes Revisited," *Scientific American*, November 1995, 26. As quoted by Wetzel, *Sexual Wisdom*, 155.

[110] E. Moberly, *Homosexuality: A New Christian Ethic* (Cambridge: James Clarke, 1983); G. van den Aardweg, *On the Origins and Treatment of Homosexuality: A Psychoanalytic Reinterpretation* (Westport, Connecticut: Praeger, 1986). As quoted by Wetzel, *Sexual Wisdom*, 156.

CONTRACEPTION

[111] St. Augustine *Marriage and Concupiscence* 1:15:17 (A.D. 419), St. John Chrysostom *Homilies on Romans* 24 (A.D. 391), and others. (www.catholic.com/library/Contraception_and_Sterilization.asp).

[112] Frank Sheed, *Society and Sanity* (New York: Sheed and Ward, 1953), 107.

[113] Cardinal Carlo Martini, *On the Body* (New York: Crossroad Publishing Co., 2000), 49.

[114] Pope Paul VI, encyclical letter, *Humanae Vitae* 17 (Of Human Life), (Boston: Pauline Books & Media, 1997).

[115] Donald DeMarco, *New Perspectives on Contraception* (Dayton, Ohio: One More Soul, 1999), 89.

[116] Pope John Paul II, apostolic exhortation, *Familiaris Consortio* 86 (The Role of the Christian Family in the Modern World), (Boston: Pauline Books & Media, 1981).

[117] R. E. J. Ryder, " 'Natural Family Planning' Effective Birth Control Supported by the Catholic Church," *British Medical Journal* 307 (18 September 1993): 723–726.

[118] Mercedes Arzú Wilson, *Love & Fertility* (Dunkirk, Maryland: Family of the Americas Foundation, 1986).

[119] *What's Wrong with Contraception?* (Cincinnati, Ohio: The Couple to Couple League International).

[120] West, *Good News About Sex and Marriage*, 179.

[121] Nona Aguilar, *No-Pill, No-Risk Birth Control* (New York: Rawson & Wade, 1980), 102.

[122] Mercedes Arzú Wilson, *Love & Family* (San Francisco: Ignatius Press, 1996), 254.

[123] Pope Paul VI, *Humanae Vitae* 21.

[124] Charlotte Hays, "Solving the Puzzle of Natural Family Planning," *Crisis*, December 2001, 15.

[125] Janet E. Smith. *Contraception, Why Not*. Audiotape of lecture by Janet E. Smith presented at meeting of the Catholic Physicians Guild at the Pontifical

College Josephinum, Columbus, Ohio, May 1994. Dayton, Ohio: One More Soul, 1999.

126 M. Blum, J. Perry, and I. Blum, "Antisperm Antibodies in Young Oral Contraceptive Users," *Advances in Contraception* 5 (1989): 41–46.

127 Department of Health and Human Services, National Institutes of Health, National Institute of Allergy and Infectious Diseases, "Scientific Evidence on Condom Effectiveness for Sexually Transmitted Disease (STD) Prevention," workshop summary, 20 July 2001.

128 U.S. Department of Health and Human Services, National Center for Health Statistics, *Family Practice News* (15–31 December 1990); Association of Reproductive Health, *American Family Physician* 48:5 (1994): 711. As quoted by Wetzel, *Sexual Wisdom*, 89.

129 The Consortium of State Physicians Resource Councils, "New Study Shows Higher Unwed Birthrates Among Sexually Experienced Teens Despite Increased Condom Use" (10 February 1999).

130 Joe S. McIlhaney Jr., M.D., *Why Condoms Aren't Safe* (Colorado Springs, Colorado: Focus on the Family, 1993), 6.

131 Mary S. Calderone, ed., *Abortion in the United States: A Conference Sponsored by the Planned Parenthood Federation of America and the New York Academy of Medicine* (New York: Harper and Row, 1958), 157.

132 "Sex Education for Bureaucrats," *Scotsman*, 29 June 1981. As quoted by Wetzel, *Sexual Wisdom*, 89.

133 Mother Teresa, 5 February 1994, National Prayer Breakfast, Washington, D.C.

134 Ryder, " 'Natural Family Planning' Effective Birth Control Supported by the Catholic Church" 723.

135 Wetzel, *Sexual Wisdom*, 273.

136 Wetzel, *Sexual Wisdom*, 274.

137 Steven Mosher, "Unto the Least of These My Brethren: U.S. Population Control Policy," *Respect Life* (Washington D.C.: United States Catholic Conference, Inc., 1998), 1.

138 Wilson, *Love & Family*, 192–193.

139 Jacqueline Kasun, "Too Many People?" *Envoy*, May–June 1998, 34.

140 Kasun, "Too Many People?" 36.

141 A. Stergachis and others, "Tubal Sterilization and the Long-term Risk of Hysterectomy," *Journal of the American Medical Association* 264 (12 December 1990): 2893–2899. As reported by *Tubal Ligation* (Cincinnati, Ohio: The Couple to Couple League International, 1995).

142 Fleet and others, *British Journal of Obstetrics and Gynecology* 95 (August 1988): 740–746. As reported by Denis St. Marie, "Sterilization, Pervasive and Insidious" (www.familyplanning.net/birth-control9.htm).

[143] The Couple to Couple League, *Tubal Ligation*.

[144] R. A. Kronmal, J. N. Kriegar, J. W. Kennedy, and others, "Vasectomy and Urolithiasis," *The Lancet* 331 (1988): 22–23. As reported in *Vasectomy* (Cincinnati, Ohio: The Couple to Couple League International, 1995).

[145] Wilson, *Love & Family*, 293.

[146] Wilson, *Love & Family*, 292.

[147] N. van der Vange, "Seven Low-dose Oral Contraceptives and Their Influence on Metabolic Pathways and Ovarian Activity" (master's thesis, Reijksuniversiteit te Utrecht, 1986), 88. As reported by Bogomir M. Kuhar, Pharm. D., *Infant Homicides through Contraceptives*, 4th ed. (Bardstown, Kentucky: Eternal Life Publishers, 2000), 42.

[148] I. Aref, F. Hefnawi, O. Kandil, M. T. Abdel Aziz, "Effect of Mini-pills on Physiologic Responses of Human Cervical Mucus, Endometrium and Ovary," *Journal of Fertility and Sterility* 24:8 (August 1973): 578–583. As reported by Nicholas Tonti-Filippini, "The Pill: Abortifacient or Contraceptive?" *Linacre Quarterly* (February 1995): 9.

[149] R. L. Kleinmann, ed., *Hormonal Contraception* (London: International Planned Parenthood Federation Medical Publications, 1990), 21; Patient package insert for Ortho-Tri-Cyclen (Raritan, New Jersey: Ortho Pharmaceutical Corporation [Johnson & Johnson], 1992). As reported by Kuhar, *Infant Homicides through Contraceptives*, 5.

[150] Robert A. Hatcher and others, *Contraceptive Technologies* (New York: Irvington Publishers, 1994), 229. As quoted by Wilson, *Love & Family*, 271.

[151] L. M. Dinerman and others, *Archives of Pediatrics and Adolescent Medicine* 149:9 (September 1995): 967–972. As reported by Westside Pregnancy Resource Center, "Teen Sex and Pregnancy: Facts and Figures."

[152] David Kingsley, "The Combined Oral Contraceptive Pill: Abortifacient and Damaging to Women" (www.lifeuk.org/speech3.html).

[153] John B. Wilks, Pharm. M.P.S., "The Pill and Breast Cancer: Your Questions Answered" (www.lifeissues.net).

[154] Chris Kahlenborn, M.D., *Breast Cancer* (Dayton, Ohio: One More Soul, 2000), 260.

[155] Kahlenborn, *Breast Cancer*, 36.

[156] I. Romieu, J. Berlin, and others, "Oral Contraceptives and Breast Cancer: Review and Meta-analysis," *Cancer* 66 (1990): 2253–2263.

[157] John B. Wilks, Pharm. M.P.S., *A Consumer's Guide to the Pill and Other Drugs*, 2nd ed. (Stafford, Virginia: American Life League, Inc., 1997), 70.

[158] Patrick McCrystal, "So They Say the Pill is Safe?" (www.hli.org/publications/hlir/1999/hr049909.html).

[159] Kahlenborn, *Breast Cancer*, 230–231; Michael Specter, "AIDS Infection and Birth Control Pills: Case of Nairobi Prostitutes Raises Questions of Pos-

sible Risk Factor," *The Washington Post*, 2 June 1987, A10.

[160] National Institute of Child Health and Human Development. *Facts About Oral Contraceptives*, by Maureen D. Gardner (www.mdadvice.com/topics/contraception_vasectomy/info/2.htm).

[161] Maureen D. Gardner, *Facts About Oral Contraceptives*.

[162] Wilks, *A Consumer's Guide to the Pill and Other Drugs*, 30.

[163] Wilks, *A Consumer's Guide to the Pill and Other Drugs*, 93–95.

[164] Blum and others, "Antisperm Antibodies in Young Oral Contraceptive Users," 41–46.

[165] S. Harlan, K. Kost, J. D. Forrest, *Preventing Pregnancy, Protecting Health* (New York: The Alan Guttmacher Institute, 1991), 98–99. As reported by "Can the Pill Kill You?" *Lovematters.com* (newspaper supplement) 4:2001:24.

[166] Johns Hopkins University, Population Information Program, *Decisions for Norplant Programs*, supplement to *Population Reports*, November 1992, 20-K:4. As reported by Wilson, *Love & Family*, 273.

[167] Thomas Hilgers, M.D., "Norplant," *Linacre Quarterly* (1993): 64–69.

[168] Wilson, *Love & Family*, 274–275.

[169] D. Taylor, "Spare the Rod," *The Guardian* (United Kingdom), 12 March 1996, 11. As quoted by Wilks, *A Consumer's Guide to the Pill and Other Drugs*, 107.

[170] E. M. Belsey, "Vaginal Bleeding Patterns among Women Using One Natural and Eight Hormonal Methods of Contraception," *Contraception* 38:2 (1988): 181–206; R. E. Lande, "New Era for Injectables," *Population Reports* 23:2-K5 (1995): 1–31. As reported by Kuhar, *Infant Homicides through Contraceptives*, 44.

[171] Wilson, *Love & Family*, 276–277.

[172] *Sexual Health Update* 7:1 (Spring 1999): 2.

[173] Kahlenborn, *Breast Cancer*, 38.

[174] Wilson, *Love & Family*, 282.

[175] Wilson, *Love & Family*, 281.

[176] Wilson, *Love & Family*, 289; Wilks, *A Consumer's Guide to the Pill and Other Drugs*, 126–128; *Sexual Health Update* 7:1 (Spring 1999): 3.

[177] Wilks, *A Consumer's Guide to the Pill and Other Drugs*, 124.

[178] Wilson, *Love & Family*, 290.

[179] "Condoms Ineffective Against Human Papilloma Virus," *Sexual Health Update* 2:2 (April 1994).

[180] R. A. Hatcher, *Contraceptive Technology, 1986–1987*, 13th ed., rev. (New York: Irvington Publishers, 1986), 139; Kim Painter, "Disturbing Data on Birth Control Failure," *USA Today*, 13 July 1989, 1D.

[181] Wilks, *A Consumer's Guide to the Pill and Other Drugs*, 136.

[182] Hillary S. Klonoff-Cohen, David A. Savitz, Robert C. Cefalo, M.D.,

Margaret F. McCann, "An Epidemiologic Study of Contraception and Pre-eclampsia," *Journal of the American Medical Association* 262:22 (8 December 1989).

[183] A. N. Gjorgov, M.D., "Barrier Contraception and Breast Cancer," *Contributions to Gynecology and Obstetrics* 8 (1980): 61.

[184] Editorial, "Semen and AIDS," *Child and Family* 21:2 (1990): 90–96.

[185] "Semen and AIDS," 91.

[186] "Semen and AIDS," 94.

[187] V. B. Green-Armytage and others, "Discussion on New Developments in the Investigation and Treatment of Sterility," *Proceedings of the Royal Society of Medicine* 36 (1943): 105–112. As quoted by "Semen and AIDS," 93.

[188] Klonoff-Cohen and others, "An Epidemiologic Study of Contraception and Preeclampsia," 3143.

[189] Gjorgov, "Barrier Contraception and Breast Cancer," 58.

[190] Ryder, " 'Natural Family Planning' Effective Birth Control Supported by the Catholic Church," 723–726.

[191] Archbishop Charles J. Chaput, O.F.M. Cap., "Of Human Life: A Pastoral Letter to the People of God of Northern Colorado on the Truth and Meaning of Married Love" 16, 22 July 1998.

[192] Pope John Paul II, remarks to President George W. Bush, 23 July 2001.

[193] O. Olatunbosun, H. Deneer, R. Pierson, "Human Papilloma Virus DNA Detection in Sperm Using Polymerase Chain Reaction," *Obstetrics and Gynecology* 97 (2001): 357–360.

SEXUALLY TRANSMITTED DISEASES

[194] John Diggs, M.D., "NIH [National Institutes of Health] Report Collapses Foundation of Comprehensive Sex Education," Abstinence Clearinghouse, 6 August 2001.

[195] Diggs, "NIH [National Institutes of Health] Report Collapses Foundation of Comprehensive Sex Education."

[196] Diggs, "NIH [National Institutes of Health] Report Collapses Foundation of Comprehensive Sex Education."

[197] E. F. Jones and J. D. Forrest, "Contraceptive Failure Rates Based on the 1988 NSFG [National Survey of Family Growth]," *Family Planning Perspectives* 24:1 (1992): 12–19; R. Hatcher and others, *Contraceptive Technology*, 17th ed. (New York: Irvington Publishers, 1998). As quoted by *STDs: The Facts* (Austin, Texas: The Medical Institute for Sexual Health, 1999).

[198] U.S. Department of Health and Human Services. "Scientific Review Panel Confirms Condoms Are Effective Against HIV/AIDS, But Epidimio-

logical Studies Are Insufficient for Other STDs," by *HHS News*, press release, 20 July 2001.

¹⁹⁹ Joe McIlhaney, M.D., *Safe Sex* (Grand Rapids, Michigan: Baker House Books, 1992), 23. As quoted by Bonacci, *Real Love*, 64.

²⁰⁰ *Sex is a Choice. Be Informed* (Grand Rapids, Michigan: The Core-Alliance Group, Inc., 2000).

²⁰¹ *Ob.Gyn. News* 28:15 (1 August 1993): 2. As quoted by Bonacci, *Real Love*, 66.

²⁰² Centers for Disease Control and Prevention (Atlanta, Georgia). *HIV/AIDS Surveillance Report, 2001* 13:2, table 33; *Cancer Facts & Figures* (Atlanta, Georgia: American Cancer Society, 2001).

²⁰³ Editorial, "Human Papillomavirus Infection," *British Medical Journal* 312 (2 March 1996): 522–523.

²⁰⁴ K. K. Holmes, P. A. Mardh, P. F. Sparling, and others, eds., *Sexually Transmitted Diseases*, 3rd ed. (New York: McGraw Hill Company, 1999), 347–359. As reported by "Human Papilloma Virus," *Sexual Health Update* 8:1 (Spring 2000): 2.

²⁰⁵ M. A. Van Ranst and others, "Taxonomy of the Human Papillomaviruses," *Papillomavirus Report* 3 (1993): 61–65. As reported by National Institutes of Health, "Scientific Evidence on Condom Effectiveness for Sexually Transmitted Disease (STD) Prevention," 23.

²⁰⁶ Wilks, *A Consumer's Guide to the Pill and Other Drugs*, 28.

²⁰⁷ Holmes and others, eds., *Sexually Transmitted Diseases,* 347–359. As reported by "Human Papilloma Virus," 2.

²⁰⁸ National Institutes of Health, "Scientific Evidence on Condom Effectiveness for Sexually Transmitted Disease (STD) Prevention," 24.

²⁰⁹ Wetzel, *Sexual Wisdom*, 43.

²¹⁰ U.S. Department of Health and Human Services (Washington, D.C.), Centers for Disease Control and Prevention (Atlanta, Georgia), *Prevention of Genital HPV Infection and Sequelae: Report of an External Consultants' Meeting* (December 1999). As quoted by *Sexual Health Update* 8:1 (Spring 2000): 3.

²¹¹ American Cancer Society, "Human Papilloma Virus (HPV)," 2002 (www.cancer.org).

²¹² *Centers for Disease Control Division of STD/HIV Prevention 1991 Annual Report,* Centers for Disease Control, 1992, 3; "Sexually Transmitted Diseases in the U.S.: Risks, Consequences and Costs," *Issues in Brief*, The Alan Guttmacher Institute, April 1994, 1. As quoted by Stanton, *Why Marriage Matters*, 40.

²¹³ Wetzel, *Sexual Wisdom*, 47.

²¹⁴ *Sexual Health Update* 7:2 (Summer 1999): 1.

²¹⁵ McIlhaney, *Safe Sex*, 102. As quoted by Bonacci, *Real Love*, 304.

[216] Sexual Health Update 7:2 (Summer 1999): 1.

[217] S. Samuels, "Chlamydia: Epidemic among America's Young," *Medical Aspects of Human Sexuality* (December 1989): 16.

[218] *Sexual Health Update* 7:2 (Summer 1999): 2.

[219] *Sexual Health Update* 7:2 (Summer 1999): 1.

[220] *Sexual Health Update* 7:2 (Summer 1999): 1.

[221] Lickona, "Sex, Love, and Character: It's Our Decision," 9.

[222] E. McAnarney and others, *Textbook of Adolescent Medicine* (Philadelphia: W. B. Saunders, 1992), 705. As quoted by Wetzel, *Sexual Wisdom*, 41.

[223] *Sexual Health Update* 7:2 (Summer 1999): 2.

[224] McIlhaney, *Safe Sex*, 100. As quoted by Bonacci, *Real Love*, 65.

[225] D. T. Fleming, G. M. McQuillan, R. E. Johnson, and others, "Herpes Simplex Virus Type 2 in the United States, 1976 to 1994," *New England Journal of Medicine* 337 (1997): 1105–1111. As quoted by *Genital Herpes* (Austin, Texas: The Medical Institute for Sexual Health, 2000).

[226] The Medical Institute for Sexual Health, *Genital Herpes*.

[227] Paul C. Reisser, M.D., *Sex and Singles: Reasons to Wait* (Colorado Springs, Colorado: Focus on the Family, 1991), 6.

[228] *Gynecologic Problems: Genital Herpes* (Washington, D.C.: American College of Obstetricians and Gynecologists, December 1985). As quoted by Bonacci, *Real Love*, 69.

[229] F. Oski, *Principles and Practice of Pediatrics* (Philadelphia: J. B. Lippincott, 1994), 787. As quoted by Wetzel, *Sexual Wisdom*, 42.

[230] *Gonorrhea* (Austin, Texas: The Medical Institute for Sexual Health, 2000).

[231] *Trichomonas* (Austin, Texas: The Medical Institute for Sexual Health, 2000).

[232] C. Everett Koop, M.D. As quoted by *Safe Sex?* (Boise, Idaho: Grapevine Publications, 1993).

[233] *How At Risk Are You?* (Chattanooga, Tennessee: AAA Women's Services, Inc., 1997).

[234] T. R. Eng and W. T. Butler, *The Hidden Epidemic: Confronting Sexually Transmitted Diseases* (Washington, D.C.: National Academy Press, 1997). As reported by *Sexual Health Update* 7:2 (Summer 1999): 1.

[235] Centers for Disease Control and Prevention, "Sexually Transmitted Disease Surveillance 1995," *Morbidity and Mortality Weekly Report* 45:53 (September 1996). As quoted by The Medical Institute for Sexual Health, *STDs: The Facts*.

[236] Blum and others, "Antisperm Antibodies in Young Oral Contraceptive Users," 41–46.

[237] *Sexual Health Update* 7:2 (Summer 1999): 3.

[238] Wilks, *A Consumer's Guide to the Pill and Other Drugs*, 30.
[239] Wilks, *A Consumer's Guide to the Pill and Other Drugs*, 38.
[240] Bonacci, *Real Love*, 126.

PURITY RENEWED

[241] McDowell, *Why Wait?*, 159–160.
[242] M. Lasswell and T. Lasswell, *Marriage and the Family* (Lexington, Massachusetts: Health, 1982). As reported by Parrott, *Saving Your Marriage Before It Starts*, 156.
[243] Sister Lucy Vertrusc, letter to religious superior. As reported by Going the Distance, *Envoy*, January–February 2000, 7.
[244] Kahlenborn, *Breast Cancer*, 22.
[245] Wilson, *Love & Family*, 298–305.
[246] McDowell, *Why Wait?*, 17.
[247] *Catechism of the Catholic Church* 2843.
[248] Hannah Arendt, *The Human Condition* (Chicago: University of Chicago Press, 1958), 237.
[249] Gresh, *And the Bride Wore White*, 150.

HOW TO STAY PURE

[250] Mother Teresa, foreword to *A Plea for Purity*, by Johann Christoph Arnold (Farmington, Pennsylvania: Plough Publishing House, 1996).
[251] Parrott, *Saving Your Marriage Before It Starts*, 145.
[252] Shalit, *A Return to Modesty*, 57.
[253] Wojtyla (Pope John Paul II), *Love and Responsibility*, 172.
[254] Michael Collopy, *Works of Love Are Works of Peace* (San Francisco: Ignatius Press, 1996), 30.
[255] Pope John Paul II, "The Opposition in the Human Heart between the Spirit and the Body," *The Theology of the Body*, 128–129.
[256] The Australian Family Association 7:1 (February 2001). As reported by *Abstinence Network* 5:1 (Spring 2001): 9.
[257] Paul M. Quay, S.J., *The Christian Meaning of Human Sexuality* (San Francisco: Ignatius Press, 1985), 106.
[258] Shalit, *A Return to Modesty*, 157.
[259] Mike Mathews, "Sexy Fashions? What Do Men Think?" *Lovematters.com* (newspaper supplement), 4:2001:10.
[260] Pope John Paul II, *Mulieris Dignitatem* 1.
[261] Mary Beth Bonacci, "Expressing Love: How to Speak the Language of Permanence," *Be*, May–June 2000, 10.

[262] Shalit, *A Return to Modesty*, 229.

[263] St. Catherine of Siena, letter 368. As referenced by Pope John Paul II address, August 2000, Rome, World Youth Day.

VOCATIONS

[264] Pope John Paul II, address, 31 May 1982, Edinburgh, Scotland. As quoted by López, ed., *The Meaning of Vocation*, 10.

[265] Pope John Paul II, address, 18 May 1988, Asuncion, Paraguay. As quoted by López, ed., *The Meaning of Vocation*, 22.

[266] Pope John Paul II, address, 13 January 1996, Manila, Philippines. As quoted by López, ed., *The Meaning of Vocation*, 23.

[267] Pope John Paul II, address, 16 October 1987, Rome, Italy. As quoted by López, ed., *The Meaning of Vocation*, 33.

[268] Pope John Paul II, *Crossing the Threshold of Hope* (New York: Alfred A. Knopf, Inc., 1994), 121.

[269] Daily report, Zenit (news agency), 4 June 2000.

[270] Pontifical Council for the Family, *The Truth and Meaning of Human Sexuality* (Boston: Pauline Books & Media, 1996), 33.